Gladstone, the Man: A Non-Political Biography

David Williamson

Photo by]   [NUMA BLANC, FILS, Cannes.

ONE OF THE LATEST PORTRAITS OF MR. GLADSTONE.

Photo'd at Cannes, February, 1898.

GLADSTONE:
THE MAN.

A NON-POLITICAL BIOGRAPHY

BY

DAVID WILLIAMSON.

ILLUSTRATED.

SECOND EDITION.

London :
JAMES BOWDEN,
10, HENRIETTA STREET, W.C.

1898.

CONTENTS.

CONTENTS

LI HUNG CHANG AND MR. GLADSTONE.

(*From a Photograph by* G. W. WEBSTER, Chester.)

Photo by]   [A. F. MACKENZIE,

MR. GLADSTONE IN 1897.

A Portrait taken in the grounds of Butterstone House, near Dunkeld.

baronet on the suggestion of Sir Robert Peel in 1845. He had married, as his second wife, Miss Robertson, daughter of a Provost of Dingwall. Her portrait has been painted in these words: " A lady of great accomplishments, of fascinating manners, of commanding presence, and high intellect ; one to grace any home, and endear any heart." There is an interesting family tree in existence which bears out Mr. Gladstone's proud boast that he had not a drop of any but Scottish blood in his veins, but Liverpool claims him gladly as one of her citizens. He was born in Rodney-street, on December 29, 1809.

not a drop but Scotch.

He was a bright child, and was encouraged to discuss freely all sorts of subjects, especially political, with his father. His brother John was likewise interested in politics, and both were destined to sit in the House of Commons, although not on the same sides of the House. Among Mr. John Gladstone's friends was George Canning, and it is not surprising that such a personality made its impression on the boy, whose bump of reverence was already developing.

with its unique life of learning. Hardly a more picturesque incident occurred in Mr. Gladstone's career than when he spent a short time, after passing his eightieth birthday, in residing within college walls at Oxford. During his 'varsity life the potent forces in the religious world of Oxford were Dr. Pusey, Dr. Whately (who subsequently became Archbishop of Dublin), and Dr. Newman, whose sermons in St. Mary's, with their indescribable charm and force, were already ruffling the waters of controversy. These men, undoubtedly, affected Gladstone's theological standpoint, although he was too thoughtful to be dominated by the most forceful intellect. Already that love of mathematical debate, if one may use the phrase, which became such a characteristic of his later years, was being developed, and he enjoyed argument for argument's sake. When Garibaldi was said to be contemplating marriage with a distinguished lady of title (although his wife was still living), it was wittily suggested that Mr. Gladstone should " explain away " the lady in question ! There is no doubt that his powers of con-

vincing himself and others were remarkable,
even in his undergraduate days. This gift
was much in request at the Union, where he
crossed swords with several future opponents
who continued the duel of words in a more
august assembly.

Gladstone's political career (concerning
which, as stated in our first sentences, we shall
have practically nothing to say) began in 1832,
when, as a Tory, he entered the House of
Commons to represent the pocket borough of
Newark. Thereafter politics ran like a thread
throughout the chain of events in his life ;
although there is concurrently the interesting
life of Gladstone as the man, which we hope
to record.

In 1832, after leaving Oxford, he paid a
visit to Italy, and the next year was shocked
to receive the news of Arthur Hallam's death
at Vienna. "I felt, wrote Mr. Gladstone,
"not only that a dear friend had been lost,
but that a great light had been extinguished,
and one who was eminently required by the
coming necessities of the country and the age.
... Whether he possessed the greatest genius I

have ever known is a question which does not lie upon my path and which I do not undertake to determine. It is of the man that I speak, and genius does not of itself make the man. When we deal with men, genius and character must be jointly taken into view; and the relation between the two, together with the effect upon the aggregate, is infinitely variable. The towering position of Shakespeare among poets does not of itself afford a certain indication that he holds a place equally high among men."

On January 13, 1833, Mr. Gladstone was admitted to the Society of Lincoln's Inn, and kept eleven terms. He had obviously at this time an intention of becoming a barrister and worked industriously with this in view, but after six years he found that his political work was absorbing his time and interests, and accordingly petitioned for the removal of his name. The exact entry on the books of the Inn is as follows :—" William Ewart Gladstone, of Christ Church, Oxford, B.A., age 23 years, fourth son of John Gladstone, Esq., of Fasque, county Kincardineshire, is admitted

into the society of this Inn the 25th day of
January, 1833.—Admitted by the Right Hon.
Sir Lancelot Shadwell, Treasurer." This was,
the observant will notice, just four days before
he signed the rolls of the House of Commons
for the first time. This further entry records
the conclusion of his career as a law student :
" At a council held the 15th day of April,
1839. Upon the petition of William Ewart
Gladstone, Esq., a Fellow of this Society,
praying that his name may be taken off the
books, having given up his intention of being
called to the Bar. It is ordered accordingly."
One may complete this reference by mentioning that about sixty years afterwards Mr.
Gladstone was the guest of the Inn on Grand
Day. He was shown his autograph as a
student, which was very slightly different from
his later signature. The old man looked at
it with a curious interest, and remarked
pathetically, " I put more into it then."

THREE GENERATIONS OF GLADSTONES.

(From a Copyright Photo by ELLIOTT & FRY.)

CHAPTER II.

HIS MARRIAGE AND FAMILY LIFE.

IN any record of Mr. Gladstone's life, an important place must be allotted to his marriage, for his long and happy union had much to do with the peace of mind which enabled him to accomplish so much public work. "Marriage is promotion," says a distinguished writer, and certainly Mr. Gladstone's was promotion in the best sense. He had often met the young lady of his choice, Miss Catherine Glynne, in London society, where she and her sister had shone as bright particular stars by reason of their beauty and intellectual charm, and he furthered their acquaintance when touring on the Continent.

The future bride was the daughter of Sir Stephen Glynne, who died when she was a child, leaving an eight-year-old son, Stephen, to

succeed him.   Lady Glynne, the widow, had
charge of the Hawarden estates during the
heir's minority, and her brother, the Hon.
George Neville, was rector.   In those days,
the village, on which so much public attention has since been fixed, enjoyed a very
bad reputation for drunkenness and disorderly
behaviour.   At last affairs reached a climax,
and the rector called a public meeting of
the Hawarden villagers, and said, " I cannot
change your hearts, that is something which
has to be done by yourselves, by the help of a
Higher than I, but I can banish the temptations
to this indecent conduct ; so I shall ask my
sister, Lady Glynne, to reduce the number of
public-houses, and to have those which remain
shut during those hours on Sunday when the
better disposed are worshipping in God's house,
of which time the worst among you take advan-
tage to behave in this most unseemly manner."
Following her brother's hint, Lady Glynne
forestalled the Welsh Sunday Closing Act, by
closing all public-houses during divine service,
and ending some altogether.   This public-
spirited lady left a marked impression on her

daughters, and much of Mrs. Gladstone's philanthropic work was, doubtless, inspired by the example of Lady Glynne.

On July 25, 1839, a double wedding made the bells of Hawarden ring out with joy; Mr. Gladstone became the husband of Catherine Glynne, and his friend, Lord Lyttelton, a man of remarkable ability, wedded her sister, amid great rejoicings.   Sir Francis Doyle, Mr. Gladstone's best man, indited a charming poem to the bride of his friend, bidding her " soothe in many a toil-worn hour, the noble heart which thou hast won."   Throughout the long years, during which she has often had to play a prominent part in social duties alien to her nature, Mrs. Gladstone was a never-failing comfort and support to her distinguished husband.   In Schiller's beautiful words, she managed to " twine and weave heavenly roses into earthly life."   Quite apart from her relationship to the man who held the Premiership of this country four times, Mrs. Gladstone would have a proper claim to notice as one of the most practical and benevolent philanthropists in the Queen's reign.   Despite considerable family cares—she was the mother of eight children—Mrs. Gladstone devoted much time, thought, and energy to many schemes of charity which benefited different classes of the community. When she was constantly in London, while her husband was engaged in Parliamentary duties, she was always engaged in benevolent schemes. She was one of the promoters of the Newport Market Refuge, which gives shelter to wanderers out of work and in misery, and aids them in gaining employment.

Mr. and Mrs. Gladstone used to spend their vacations at Hawarden, where her brother, Sir Stephen Glynne, was in residence. They had more than one family sorrow, losing a little daughter, and sustaining a severe bereavement by the death of Lord Lyttelton, whose talented widow, it is interesting to remember, became one of the instructresses of the Queen.

The names of Mr. and Mrs. Gladstone's children may be stated conveniently here. The eldest son was William Henry, who married a daughter of Lord Blantyre. He was studious and musical, composing many hymn tunes which have found a place in

MR. GLADSTONE'S STUDY.

(*From a Photo by Mr. F. THURSTON, Luton.*)

various collections. For some years he was the unobtrusive representative of East Worcestershire in the House of Commons. To the great grief of his relatives Mr. Gladstone died, after a comparatively short illness, in 1891. His widow and family reside at Hawarden, and the estates will ultimately devolve upon his son William, whose only public appearance so far was as train-bearer to the Prince of Wales when he attended the opening of the new University of Wales. Mr. W. H. Gladstone had built Hawarden House near to the Castle, and resided there, under an arrangement that his father and mother should retain the Castle during their life. He was fifty-one years old at the time of his death. Among the letters of sympathy received concerning this event by Mr. Gladstone was one penned by Mrs. Spurgeon on behalf of her famous husband, the preacher, who was then lying seriously ill.

The eldest daughter, Anne, is the wife of the Rev. Dr. E. Wickham, who held the headmastership of Wellington College for some years, and is now Dean of Lincoln.

The Rev. Stephen Edward Gladstone is the second son ; he has been rector of Hawarden for some years.

The third son is Mr. Henry Neville Gladstone, who was resident in India until lately, being connected with an important mercantile house. His wife was the Hon. Maud Ernestine Rendel, daughter of Lord Rendel, who was formerly chairman of the Welsh Party in the House of Commons.

The youngest son is the Right Hon. Herbert John Gladstone, aged forty-four, who is unmarried. He was educated at Eton and Oxford, taking a first class in modern history, and was lecturer on modern history at Keble College for some years. After sustaining defeat in an attempt to win a Liberal seat in Middlesex, he was chosen in 1880 to represent Leeds, which had returned his father to Parliament. Mr. Herbert Gladstone acted as private secretary to the Prime Minister, and was a Junior Lord of the Treasury. Since then he has held the offices of Financial Secretary of War, Under-Secretary for Home Affairs, and First Commissioner of Works. In the last eighteen years Leeds has been loyal to him at various contested elections. He inherits a beautiful voice from his father, and is an expert platform orator. He has modestly refrained from speaking much in the House of Commons; but he showed excellent administrative ability when he held office. Very fond of music, and a pleasant vocalist, he had been a member of the Handel Society for some years. "Mr. Herbert," as the villagers of Hawarden call him, was a great athlete in his younger days, and has shown his interest in sport by supporting generously the National Physical Recreation Society, of which he was president. He gave £1,000 to the Hawarden Institute, which has been of incalculable benefit in promoting athletics and culture among the youths of the neighbourhood. Once he was asked what recreations his father took, and replied: "He used to be chiefly fond of rowing, riding, and shooting; but during the last twenty or twenty-five years he had to give up those forms of exercise, and to confine himself mainly to cutting down trees, which he did habitually. He always was a

great walker, and lost no opportunity of
encouraging his sons in physical recreation ;
but it was only in manly sports and games, in
rational recreations that he stimulated and led
us." I came across the following apt pen-
portrait of Mr. Herbert Gladstone, in these
lines by George Crabbe, in his poem entitled
" The Hall of Justice " :

> A sturdy youth he was and tall,
> His looks would all his soul declare ;
> His piercing eyes were deep and small,
> And strongly curl'd his raven hair.
>
> *   *   *   *   *
>
> His father was our party's chief.

The third daughter in the Gladstone family
is Mary, better known to the public as Mrs.
Harry Drew. She was always an alert reader,
and was one of the first to recognise the
literary abilities of " Lanoe Falconer," whose
first book, it may be remembered, " Made-
moiselle Ixe," received enthusiastic commenda-
tion from Mr. Gladstone. Mrs. Drew possesses
considerable powers herself as a writer, and
after her marriage she spent much of her
time in lightening the literary labours of her
father. She and her husband live at Buckley, a

parish which is not far from Hawarden; Mr. Drew is Warden of St. Deiniol's Hostel, of which Mrs. Drew is treasurer and one of the trustees. Their daughter Dorothy interested the public greatly by her youthful charm when she accompanied her grandparents in their drives about London. The little girl, with her golden locks and blue eyes, made a charming note of juvenility amid the official dinginess of 10, Downing-street. At least one Cabinet Minister can remember the sudden and unexpected patter of little feet behind him on the stairs, and the unceremonious greeting of Dorothy, who had small respect for politicians, but much for playmates. The little lady, who has been in danger of being "spoilt" by so much notice, was accorded the special honour of a private introduction to the Queen. Some of her remarks to Her Majesty, if wanting in formality, were amusing in their originality. The Queen was charmed with the child. Another incident in Dorothy Drew's already eventful career was when she acted as a bridesmaid to her kind friend, Miss Margot Tennant, on her marriage to Mr. Asquith. Mr. Glad-

stone's partiality for Dorothy was well known,
and her bright naïveté helped to dispel many
of the anxious cares which weighed on him
in his last Premiership. I well remember the
scene of the final departure of Mr. and Mrs.
Gladstone from the official home in Downing-
street, which at intervals they had occupied
so long. It was a dull afternoon; the news
as to the Premier's resignation was still await-
ing confirmation, so that few people had any
idea that a historic incident was taking place
in the quiet little street which branches off
Whitehall. A small group of reporters stood
opposite the house, with their note-books and
pencils ready to chronicle the details of the
right hon. gentleman's departure. Presently
the door opened, and Mr. Gladstone, wearing
a thick overcoat and Inverness cape, issued
forth, and began promenading the pavement
with rapid steps. His head was bent, and his
face seemed wrapt in thought.

> Even the bravest heart must swell
> At the moment of farewell.

Soon he turned to the door as it opened,
and with old-world gallantry he aided Mrs.

Gladstone to enter the brougham. Then running down the steps and smiling with glee
came little Dorothy Drew, delighted with the
prospect of a drive with her grandparents, and
quite unaware that she was a participant in a
notable scene in the career of a Prime Minister.
She gaily waved her little hand while Mr.
Gladstone bowed gravely in acknowledgment
of the respectful salutations of the members of
the Press, who had seen him on so many public
occasions. In a minute the carriage bearing
the Prime Minister and his wife on their way
to Paddington had passed out of sight, and
Downing-street had bidden farewell to its most
famous resident.

That is a reminiscence which concerns one
of the grandchildren of Mr. Gladstone, but it
must not be forgotten that there are others—
Mr. W. H. Gladstone's children—who have
been a joy in the declining years of the Grand
Old Man. A photograph exists of Mr.
Gladstone with his grandson William on his
knee, a charming contrast between old age
and youth.

With a brief allusion to the little daughter,

Catherine Jessy, who died in infancy, this record
of the family life of Mr. Gladstone may close.
Of his eight children, six survive, each
endowed with gifts which have been already,
and will continue to be, serviceable in perpe-
tuating with honour the name they bear

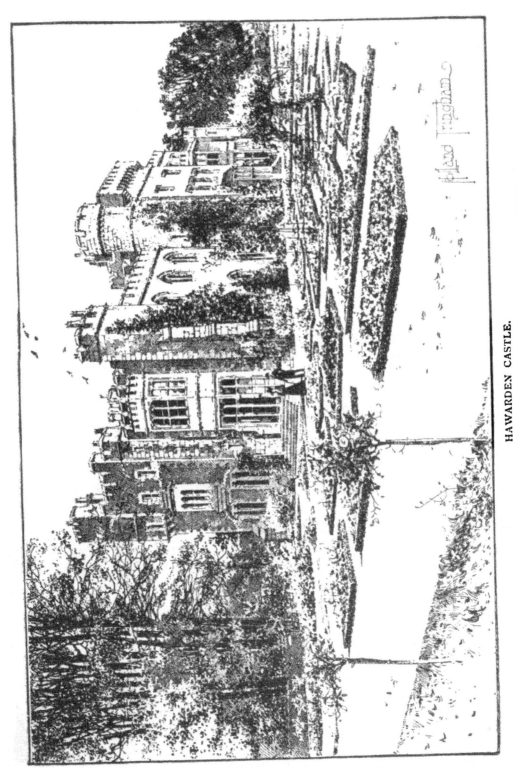

HAWARDEN CASTLE.

(*Drawn by* HOLLAND TRINGHAM *from a Photo by* G. W. WILSON & CO.)

CHAPTER III.

HIS WORK AS AN AUTHOR.

IT is time that something should·be said about Mr. Gladstone's remarkable literary labours, which may be said to have commenced with the publication of "The State in its Relation to the Church," published in the autumn of 1838. The titlepage bore the inscription "By W. E. Gladstone, Student of Christ Church, and M.P. for Newark." The book was dedicated to the author's *alma mater*, the University of Oxford, which he described as "The fountain of blessings, spiritual, social, and intellectual." Mr. Gladstone's power of argument and his love of ecclesiastical history were shown forcibly in the pages of this book. The volume attracted so much attention ·that a second edition was made necessary very speedily. With the leisure which distinguished that period, in con-

trast to the haste with which reviews appear on
the identical day of publication, it was about
a year before either of the great reviews noticed
the book. But when *The Quarterly Review* did
take the subject in hand, it treated the book
with consummate power in a review of fifty-
five pages. In the course of this, the writer
paid the author several compliments, such as,
" He is evidently not an ordinary character,
though it is to be hoped that many others are
now forming themselves in the same school
with him, to act hereafter on the same
principle. And the highest compliment which
we can pay him is to show that we believe him
to be what a statesman or philosopher should
be—indifferent to his own reputation for
talents, and only anxious for truth and right,"

More familiar than is the book itself to
modern readers is the brilliant review by
Macaulay which appeared in *The Edinburgh*
prior to *The Quarterly's* review. The two men
stood in very similar relationship to the world
in which they were destined to play so
prominent a part, for Macaulay had secured
the same extraordinary success at Cambridge

as Mr. Gladstone had attained at Oxford. Both were attracted almost as equally to literature as to politics, and both were concerned seriously with the matters of life. Mr. Gladstone could not help feeing very grateful to the anonymous, but obvious reviewer in the *Edinburgh*, and put his feelings into a letter written from 6, Carlton-gardens, where he was then residing. This epistle was expressed in humble phrases, which, undoubtedly, gave pleasure to its recipient, who quite realised his own importance with the world of literature. Thus was the foundation-stone laid of that monument of literary activity to which Mr. Gladstone was adding almost every year of his life.

His next most forcible publication was the famous "Letter to the Earl of Aberdeen," which described most graphically and truthfully the fearful atrocities perpetrated in the dungeons of Naples. The details for this letter were obtained by Mr. Gladstone when he was visiting Italy in 1850, and he collected them with painstaking energy. The letter, which bore on its face the stamp of evident truth, caused quite a sensation in Europe, and the author published a second, containing fuller details. It was discussed in Parliament, and drew from Lord Palmerston a forcible statement on the subject. In the course of his speech the Foreign Secretary said :—" Mr. Gladstone has done himself, as I think, very great honour by the course he pursued at Naples, and by the course he has followed since ; for I think that when you see an English gentleman, who goes to pass a winter at Naples —instead of confining himself to those amusements that abound in that city—instead of diving into volcanoes and exploring excavated cities—when we see him going to courts of justice, visiting prisons, descending into dungeons, and examining great numbers of unfortunate victims of illegality and injustice, with a view afterwards to enlist public opinion in the endeavour to remedy those abuses—I think that it is a course that does honour to the person that pursues it ; and concurring in opinion with him that the influence of public opinion in Europe might have some useful effect in setting such matters right, I thought it my duty to send copies of his pamphlet to our Ministers at the various Courts of Europe, directing them to give to each Government copies of the pamphlet, in the hope that, by affording them an opportunity of reading it, they might be led to use their influence for promoting what is the object of my honourable and gallant friend—a remedy for the evils to which he has referred."

An undoubted stimulus was given to Mr. Gladstone's interest in Greece, both ancient and modern, by his acceptance of the office of Lord High Commissioner Extraordinary to the Ionian Isles. There had been considerable trouble in these islands, which for forty-three years had been under British Protectorate. Sir John Young, who was Lord High Commissioner of them, had lately recommended the conclusion of this Protectorate, except as regards Corfu, which he advised should remain a military station. This despatch was published, to the surprise of the Government of Lord Palmerston, in *The Daily News*, towards the end of 1858. As there was a good deal of difference in opinion in the matter of retaining

c

the Ionian Isles, whose inhabitants to some extent were favouring the idea of union with Greece, it was thought an excellent plan to send Mr. Gladstone to report on the state of affairs. According to his manner, he lost no time in making himself fully acquainted with the position, and, having conducted his mission, returned to this country. The Greeks always had a high respect for him from their first acquaintance, and I can remember the late Monsieur Tricoupis, Prime Minister of Greece, telling me, as he paced up and down his library at Athens, how enthusiastic a crowd of Greeks would still become were the name of Gladstone uttered.

Before Mr. Gladstone's visit to the Ionian Islands, he had published a book entitled "The Place of Homer in Classical Education and Historical Inquiry," and this was followed by "Studies of Homer in the Homeric Age," which contains his views as to the Homeric Theo-mythology. Another literary production was a share in a volume of translations from Homer, Æschylus, Horace, Catullus, Dante, and other classics. His colleague in this book was Lord Lyttelton, his friend, who was never happier than when perusing his favourite Greek and Latin authors.

In 1863 he collected his Budget speeches, *5*, and the excellence of phrasing, as well as that rare ability to "set figures to music" which distinguished them, gained for the book high admiration from critics.

The activities of politics kept Mr. Gladstone's pen idle soon afterwards, although he found time to write an admirable review of "Ecce *6.* Homo," a book by Mr. Sidgwick, which was then being much discussed. This review appeared first in *Good Words*, and was reprinted. "A Chapter of Autobiography" and "Juventus Mundi" were published in 1869. Then for some time he was so much engaged in State affairs that literature had to remain in the background, save as regards the omnivorous reading of new books. The growth of reviews was especially noticeable about 1874, when to *The Fortnightly Review* were added new rivals in the shape of *The Contemporary Review* and *The Nineteenth Century*. Mr. Gladstone contributed to both new organs of public opinion, several articles covering a wide field of subjects, ranging from "Russian Policy" to "Ritualism." In 1874, there appeared his noteworthy pamphlet on the "Vatican Decrees," which excited much public discussion. Later on, when the Bulgarian atrocities were at their height, he roused the world with his pamphlets on that sorrowful subject, which possessed his soul quite as intensely as the more recent occurrences in Armenia.

After his retirement from a "laborious public life," as he termed it in his letter to the Earl of Granville in 1875, he was able to devote more time to literary studies. One result of this leisure was an interesting article in *The British Quarterly Review* on the Evangelical Movement, and a collection of articles under the title of "Gleanings of Past Years." It may be mentioned that the latter volume was a favourite wedding present from Mr. Gladstone, and not a few bridegrooms who now stand high in the world of politics and society possess a copy with the right honourable gentleman's autograph inscription. It

MR. GLADSTONE IN 1887.

would be impossible and unnecessary to summarise fully all Mr. Gladstone's literary labours, which continued down to the latest years of his life ; but a series of articles under the title of "The Impregnable Rock of Holy Scripture," which appeared in *Good Words* in 1890, demands attention for its singular nobility of eloquence, and its wide range of inquiry into the opinions and doubts of others. Mr. Gladstone was greatly interested in the position maintained by Professor Huxley on the subject of the Gadarene swine and allied Scriptural themes. To the last he was always prepared for conversation on theological subjects, and more than one story is told regarding his enjoyment of such themes. When the Revised Version of the New Testament was published, a former private secretary said to Mr. Gladstone that it was distinctly inferior to the Authorised Version. "Indeed," replied Mr. Gladstone, his eye glistening with the anticipation of a theological debate, "I am very much interested to hear you say so. Pray give me an instance." "Well," replied his friend, "look at the first verse of the second chapter

of St. Luke, which used to run : ' There went
out a decree from Cæsar Augustus that all the
world should be taxed.'   Now I always thought
that a splendid idea—a tax levied on the whole
world by a single act—a grand decree worthy
of a great empire and an Imperial Treasury !
But in the Revised Version I find the words,
' There went out a decree that all the world
should be enrolled '—a mere counting, a
census, the sort of thing the Local Government
Board might do ! Will anyone convince me
that the new version is as good as the old one
in this passage ? "

Mr. Gladstone used to revel in discussion
with learned scholars such as Dr. Döllinger, the
aged representative of the Old Catholic school,
Dr. Ginsburg, Lord Acton, and others, on
theology, which was also a favourite theme of
conversation with his physician, the late Sir
Andrew Clark.   It was a singular proof of the
magnetic charm of Mr. Gladstone's conversation
that on whatever subject he chose to discourse
he could always be sure of listeners. And one
found oneself easily involved in eager attention
to a dialectical duel on the most abstruse topic.

It would be almost impossible to compile a complete Gladstone bibliography, for the mere enumeration of Mr. Gladstone's publications fill a great space in the British Museum catalogue. After he passed his eightieth birthday, he continued with wonderful industry his investigations into Homeric study. He delivered the Romanes Lecture in 1892, and, besides writing on special aspects of the Irish question, he was deep in the study of Bishop Butler's works, which he edited with scholarly ability in 1896. Once again he showed his interest in the defence of the Scriptures by contributing a splendid essay on "The Value of Scriptural Studies to the Laity" to the People's Bible History, from which we extract this exquisite concluding passage :—"'Heaven and earth shall pass away, but My words shall not pass away.' As they have lived and wrought, so they will live and work. From the teacher's chair and from the pastor's pulpit; in the humblest hymn that ever mounted to the ear of God from beneath a cottage roof, and in the rich, melodious choir of the noblest cathedral, 'their sound is gone out into all lands, and

their words unto the ends of the world.' Nor
here alone, but in a thousand silent and
unsuspected forms will they unweariedly
prosecute their holy office. Who doubts that,
times without number, particular portions of
Scripture find their way to the human soul as if
embassies from on high, each with its own
commission of comfort, of guidance, or of
warning ? What crisis, what trouble, what
perplexity of life has failed or can fail to draw
from this inexhaustible treasure-house its proper
supply ? What profession, what position
is not daily and hourly enriched by these
words which repetition never weakens, which
carry with them now, as in the days of their
first utterance, the freshness of youth and
immortality ? When the solitary student opens
all his heart to drink them in, they will reward
his toil. And in forms yet more hidden and
withdrawn, in the retirement of the chamber,
in the stillness of the night season, upon the
bed of sickness, and in the face of death, the
Bible will be there, its several words how often
winged with their several and special messages,
to heal and to soothe, to uplift and uphold, to

invigorate and stir. Nay, more, perhaps, than this; amid the crowds of the court, or the forum, or the street, or the market-place, when every thought of every soul seems to be set upon the excitements of ambition, or of business, or of pleasure, there too, even there, the still small voice of the Holy Bible will be heard, and the soul, aided by some blessed word, may find wings like a dove, may flee away and be at rest."

He published a fervid letter to the Duke of Westminster on the Armenian question in March, 1897, to which widespread circulation was given by its being reprinted in *The Daily Chronicle*. In connection with Mr. Gladstone's revival of interest in Bishop Butler, it is interesting to record that his old friend Lord Northbourne signified his intention of placing a tablet in Durham Cathedral to the memory of the author of the famous Analogy, who was bishop of the diocese for two years. For this tablet Mr. Gladstone wrote the inscription. Mention has already been made of the article, "Personal Recollections of Arthur H. Hallam," which Mr. Gladstone wrote for publication in

1898 in *The Youth's Companion*—an appreciation as fine as exists in the English language.

It is fitting that the last volumes which bear Mr. Gladstone's name should be those connected with theology, just as his earliest literary success was gained in the same field. Amid all the examples of statesmen who have also been authors, William Ewart Gladstone stands out paramount for prolific labours of authorship touching so many subjects of human interest.

CHAPTER IV.

HIS ORATORY.

AFTER discussing the more permanent pen labours of Mr. Gladstone, we may touch on the magnificent speeches which influenced public opinion and impressed multitudes with the strongest belief in the man who uttered them. Probably no man in the century was seen and heard by so many hundreds of thousands of his countrymen. He was one of those orators who possessed remarkable powers of adaptability to any audience. No public function at which he spoke—an open-air political gathering, a learned lecture in ancient Oxford, a luncheon party attended by Royalty on board the *Tantallon Castle*, or a gathering of Free Church ministers to listen to his views on preaching— was disappointed with Mr. Gladstone's speech. It was always eloquent, always rang with the

note of sincerity, and was always suggestive.
No man probably ever started so much
discussion as he ; no speaker was such a boon
to leader-writers in initiating new topics.

Apart from his set orations, delivered on
political campaigns, with a fervour that set the
heather on fire, one has to note the admirable
series of speeches on all sorts of subjects, such
as pottery, fruit culture, and kindred themes.
The right hon. gentleman was always at his
best at the annual fête held in Hawarden Park,
and many have been the memorable and
delightful speeches which he has delivered to
his friends and neighbours. An address quite
by itself in impressiveness was that which he
gave to the boys at Mill Hill School several
years ago, certainly never to be forgotten by any
who heard it.

He was a marvellously copious orator, and
when once he became interested in his subject,
lost, as did also his hearers, all account of time.
On one occasion his physician had forbidden
him to exceed an hour, but that period had
long been passed ere he concluded his speech.
His voice gathered volume as it went along,

REDUCED FACSIMILE OF THE "NATIONAL LIBERAL" GOLDEN WEDDING
ADDRESS, 1889.

and there was no need for even the deafest to
shout "Speak up!" His <u>face</u> while he was
speaking was particularly interesting, because
his features reflected so quickly the alternate
play of <u>seriousness</u> and <u>humour</u>. Of course,
Mr. Gladstone's <u>humour was always of a
subtle character.</u> Indeed, sometimes his mere
quotations from the classics, though their
meaning might be hidden to the majority of
his audience, would cause great laughter,
because their humorous or apt allusions would
be guessed by the dramatic force with which
they were delivered. He was undoubtedly a
<u>consummate actor.</u> His sentences were often
remarkably involved ; one, I remember, contained 217 words, yet was perfectly clear if
read slowly. He often used "alliteration's
artful aid." I recollect finding in a speech
which he delivered in 1887 the following
examples of it :—"shielded and sheltered";
"persistent pursuit"; "refractory and recal-
citrant"; "reasonable and rational." His
rate of speed varied considerably, attaining
sometimes to <u>160 words a minute,</u> but was
generally below that rate. Reporters found Mr.

Gladstone comparatively easy to follow, as his sentences, however lengthy, concluded properly in the end.   Mr. Gladstone was exceedingly thoughtful in aiding the arduous labours of the Press whenever he could ; and sometimes, if a too enthusiastic audience drowned the conclusion of a sentence with applause, he would lean forward and repeat it for the benefit of the reporters.   Considering the immense amount of space which his speeches have occupied in the newspapers, the correctness with which they have been reported is remarkable.   He had a high view of the usefulness of shorthand, which he considered, if judiciously employed, was "a most valuable auxiliary to self-education."   On the occasion of his Midlothian campaigns the arrangements for telegraphing his speeches were on the most elaborate scale, and, understanding their importance, all the members of the Press were on their mettle.

Before making a great speech Mr. Gladstone liked to be left alone in quietude.   Mr. John Morley once said to Matthew Arnold, "Whenever I travel, I carry a volume of your writings with me. Before making a speech, I read it for inspiration, and afterwards, I read it again for consolation." But Mr. Gladstone would have read more probably Dante or Homer than a modern poet.

As a rule, he used very few notes, and these *14* of the simplest character. I have had the pleasure of examining the notes used by him on the occasion of the introduction of his Home Rule Bill. Considering the complications of that measure, the maze of details through which he glided with the ease of experience, these half-sheets of paper were a remarkable tribute to Mr. Gladstone's possession of the whole case in his mind while addressing the House of Commons. His finest short speeches were undoubtedly those which commemorated the deaths of his great rival, Lord Beaconsfield, Lord Iddesleigh, Lord F. Cavendish, John Bright, the Emperor Frederick, and the Duke of Albany. After Mr. Gladstone had voiced the House of Commons on such occasions, no subsequent speaker could possibly add anything without breaking *15* the spell. Take, for instance, the peroration of

his speech on the tragic death of the Emperor
Frederick. "So far as human sorrow can be
alleviated, either by the expression of
sympathy or glorious recollections, or by yet
more glorious hopes, all that consolation will
be enjoyed by those who are now mourning
over the death of the German Emperor. But
one thing remains to those, and it is this—the
recollection of his great qualities, of his
singular union of wisdom with virtue and with
valour, his known attachment to the liberties
of his country, and his respect for its constitution—all those winning qualities, and a
fortitude greater in degree than that of many a
soldier, and perhaps, of many a martyr—all
those things constitute a great and noble
inheritance for the German people : and we
trust that that great nation will treasure the
recollection of the Emperor whom they have
lost as amongst the most precious possessions
that can fall to the lot of any people upon
earth."

Everyone who has heard many of Mr.
Gladstone's speeches will have his or her
favourite. Not long ago Sir Arthur Arnold

quoted these words, which he considered the noblest and most memorable in the copious authorship of Mr. Gladstone :—"I care not to ask if there be dregs or tatters of human life such as can escape from the description and boundary of morals. I submit that duty is a power which rises with us in the morning, and goes to rest with us at night. It is co-extensive with the action of our intelligence. It is the shadow which cleaves to us, go where we will, and which only leaves us when we leave the light of life."

There was particular pathos about the last speech of Mr. Gladstone in London. It was at a crowded meeting, held in Prince's Hall, Piccadilly—since turned into a restaurant. The occasion was a meeting to initiate a memorial fund in connection with the late Sir Andrew Clark, who had been Mr. Gladstone's physician and friend for many years. When the veteran orator arrived, he was very warmly greeted by the great audience. The Duke of Cambridge (as President of the London Hospital, where Sir Andrew Clark had laboured so long) made a brief speech in support of the memorial. Then

followed Mr. Gladstone ; but for the first time
in his long career as a public speaker he was
compelled to remain seated during the delivery
of his finely phrased eulogy of him whom
George Eliot called "the beloved physician."
Mr. Gladstone paid a beautiful tribute to the
qualities of his late friend, and to the characteristics of the medical profession, which he
always admired intensely.   The scene was
touching in its unique character.   There was
the aged statesman with his noble white head,
the centre of a group of distinguished men—
Cardinal Vaughan, Sir James Paget, Mr.
Jonathan Hutchinson, Canon Wilberforce, and
many another.   From his lips came the stately
sentences in flowing rhythm, and in tones
which grew in strength as the speech pro-
gressed.   The eyes of the venerable orator had
lost some of their lustre, the voice some of its
mellifluous tones ; but the art, the passion, the
sincerity, the nobility were untouched by time.

Carlyle called Mr. Gladstone "the man
with the unmeasurable power of vocables,"
to which Tennyson retorted, "I love the man,
but no Prime Minister ought to be an orator."

Of course, his fluency laid him open to the charge of delaying business in the House of Commons. His power of persuading himself and others of the propriety of a course of action was satirised by Laurence Oliphant, in his brilliant novel, "Piccadilly." He made Lord Frank Vanecourt, who had become involved both matrimonially and financially, say of Gladstone, speaking in Parliament :— "Ah," thought I, as I gazed on that brilliant and ingenious orator, "he is the only man in the House, who, if he was in such a mess as I am, would find a way out of it." It was a great temptation to Mr. Gladstone to interpose in any debate which interested him, and Mr. Justin McCarthy has told us how he could fascinate the House of Commons with even a dissertation on Spanish corks. Mr. Tim Healy said not long ago, on this very subject of the provocation to which Mr. Gladstone fell an easy victim, that Lord Randolph Churchill could always manage to draw a speech from Mr. Gladstone, who, continued Mr. Healy, made Randolph. He saw that he had more ability and courage than the whole crowd of front-bench men behind whom he sat, and so never did Randolph rise to speak than up jumped Gladstone to answer him. Gladstone "glasshoused him." The aptness of the phrase "glasshoused" will be apparent to all who know the circumstances of the case.

A very clever parody of Mr. Gladstone's manner of speaking in the House of Commons appeared in "Barney Geoghegan, M.P.," by the versatile and brilliant writer, Mr. Edward Jenkins, author of "Ginx's Baby"; but, as it is of little value apart from its context, I must refer [my readers to the book itself, which is most amusing to all those who are interested in Parliamentary life.

Mr. Gladstone's oratory was *sui generis*. It was more ornate than the simple eloquence of John Bright, and more involved in construction. He rarely troubled to condense, but preferred to explain his ideas at length and often with tautology. But his speeches read almost equally well as they sounded, although the charm of the orator is wanting. And what a charm was his! The writer has read every line of Mr. Gladstone's speeches during

THE MISSES GLYNNE (AFTERWARDS LADY LYTTLETON
AND MRS. W. E. GLADSTONE).
(*A Photo by* G. WATMOUGH WEBSTER *of the original by* GEORGE RICHMOND.)

nearly twenty years, and was privileged to
listen to many of them both in the House of
Commons and at public gatherings. Of his
later Parliamentary efforts—quite distinct in
form and style from those delivered at his
zenith—he regards the speech introducing the
Religious Disabilities Bill as one of the most
successful. The House was crowded, and Mr.
Gladstone had a specially congenial audience
to address, for the subject was outside the
general arena of politics. How well he
used his opportunity will be seen on reference to the reports; but they can only give a
faint idea of the delightful ease of gesture,
the amiable smiles which again and again
flitted across Mr. Gladstone's face, the solemn
earnestness and pathos with which he concluded his peroration. "While he is speaking,"
said an old member of the House, "we are all
under the spell of the magician; it is only
when the thrilling tones of that marvellous
voice have ceased that we go into the division
lobbies and vote against Mr. Gladstone."

Few speeches in recent years may be said to
have altered the opinions of members. But

among these few, three or four of Mr. Gladstone's have a place.   It was certainly a
consummate success that he scored when he
asked and obtained, without a dissentient
voice, some millions of money, voted on
account of the Penjdeh incident.   Many of
his speeches contained little pieces of autobiography, full of interest, and sometimes start-
ling, in their clear recollection of events long
past.   To hear Mr. Gladstone remark, " I
remember Lord Melbourne saying," or " Mr.
Daniel O'Connell once said in my hearing,"
sent the mind wandering back to old, forgotten, far-off days, when, instead of the
aged orator, there stood in the House a handsome man in the prime of life.

Short or long—and they were often very long
—Mr. Gladstone's speeches were always worth
hearing ; and in them were always some
" purple patches " of real eloquence.   When
he spoke in the library of the National
Liberal Club and made an appeal for volumes
to fill its shelves, there was apparent the bookman's zeal ; when he pleaded for the cause of
charity, sincere sympathy with suffering was

evident; when he responded at the Mansion
House for Her Majesty's Ministers, there was
the strong sense of responsibility.   Behind
all the speeches, whenever and wherever
delivered, there shone the bright light of a
great personality, and the radiance of this light
was never dimmed even in Mr. Gladstone's
last days.

CHAPTER V.

AN OMNIVOROUS READER.

It was natural that a man who wrote so much himself should be also a great reader. Mr. Gladstone wasted little time on newspapers, although he provided them with so much material. In this respect, he held the record, for not a day passed without some use of his name either in leading articles, in reports and speeches, or in paragraphs. But for his knowledge of newspaper matters he depended much on other people's reading. He once said to a friend that he scarcely read *The Times*, except for the purpose of perusing the foreign intelligence. He used to read *The Daily News*, and *The Pall Mall Gazette*, in its old days; latterly, he was a daily reader of *The Westminster Gazette*. In this matter of eschewing daily papers, he has had a follower in the person of Mr. A. J. Balfour, who has again and again confessed his ignorance of what "the papers" say. The time saved from ephemeral publications, Mr. Gladstone devoted to books. He liked to keep three volumes, each differing entirely in subject from the other, before him at the same time; turning from one with renewed interest in the other. It was stated by Miss Hulda Friederichs that after Mr. Gladstone had been reading strenuously Bishop Butler's works, he would take up the "Arabian Nights' Entertainments" or "Robinson Crusoe's Travels" as a change of literary pasture. This was a similar idea to the plan of farmers who do not expect two successive harvests of wheat from the same ground; and there is little doubt that by interspersing his more serious studies with light fiction he managed to accomplish much more than the man who confined himself solely to solid volumes.

Mr. Gladstone was ever ready to read a new book up to within a year or two of his death. And when he derived pleasure from any volume, he was just as ready to express his appreciation to the author. His " post-cards " became quite a feature with publishers, who were delighted to advertise Mr. Gladstone's opinion on any book. It was partly from a sense of courtesy, partly from his respect for literature, that led Mr. Gladstone to thank even the most obscure author. Many a writer has found, with the joy of the unexpected, a cordial sentence or two of thanks from "the busiest man in Europe," written on a post-card by " your faithful servant, W. E. Gladstone." If there were any points of controversy raised in a volume, Mr. Gladstone would find time to discuss them at length, but always in the most courteous and deferential spirit. He must have reviewed, in this manner, thousands of books, besides those on which he wrote essays in *The Nineteenth Century*, and other reviews. It was wonderful how he managed to turn from the consideration of a weighty and critical question of State to the perusal of the last popular novel.

I remember seeing Robert Louis Stevenson's " Treasure Island " in Mr. Gladstone's hand, when he was on his way to Osborne to kiss hands as Prime Minister. This ability to change the current of his thoughts was undoubtedly of the utmost value to the brain of Mr. Gladstone. Sometimes he would surprise a friend who had sat silent, expecting to hear Mr. Gladstone express an opinion on some important subject, with a remark on what would be considered an insignificant matter. Thus, for instance, the late Professor Henry Drummond was his companion on one occasion, driving from London to Dollis Hill, where the Earl of Aberdeen was entertaining the Gladstones. Imagining that Mr. Gladstone's silence during the drive was due to his anxiety on public affairs, he remained silent himself all the journey. The next day Mr. Gladstone remarked casually that he had been busy calculating the number of vehicles of various sorts which passed the carriage, and had formed a clear idea of the average per mile. While mentioning their stay at Dollis Hill, one may interpolate a little story in connection with it. The late Archbishop of Canterbury and Mrs. Benson received an invitation to dine, dated from Dollis Hill, and accepted it. When the evening arrived, they drove out to Willesden, only to discover that in the meantime the Gladstones had returned to town. They had forgotten to state in the invitation that the dinner-party would be held in London, and not at Dollis Hill!

But, returning to the subject of new books, there is no doubt that Mr. Gladstone's welcome to certain volumes had much to do with their success. He was one of the first to praise "John Inglesant," a book which was actually read in MS. and declined by that experienced "taster," the late Mr. James Payn. Stories "with a purpose," even if the purpose was hardly achieved, found favour with Mr. Gladstone. Consequently, he esteemed highly the novels of "Edna Lyall," especially that in which the Irish Question played a prominent part. "To Right the Wrong" was another which he praised unstintingly. His love of historical novels never left him, and the "Wizard of the North" always charmed him. He was less fond of Thackeray and Dickens than Sir Walter Scott, whose best novels he

PORTRAIT OF MR. GLADSTONE AS A YOUNG MAN, BY LAWRENCE.
A Picture in SIR ROBERT PEEL'S *Collection, photo'd by* RUSSELL.

considered were "The Bride of Lammer-moor" and "Kenilworth."

So many opinions did he pass on books of current interest that an enterprising newspaper might have acquired an attractive column weekly, composed simply of Mr. Gladstone's reviews. Publishers, as well as authors, sent him hundreds, nay, thousands of books, and whenever he was interested in any, there was sure to be a post-card of thanks. Many of these volumes he did not preserve in his own select library after reading, for they would have soon swamped even the capacious shelves arranged on Mr. Gladstone's own adroit plan of accommodation. St. Deiniol's Library, which he established near the old church at Hawarden, possesses already 30,000 volumes, many of them having been conveyed thither by Mr. Gladstone himself. The trustees of this library include the Rev. Stephen E. Gladstone, Mr. Henry N. Gladstone, the Countess Grosvenor, Sir Walter Phillimore (the judge), the Hon. Mrs. W. H. Gladstone, and the Rev. Harry and Mrs. Drew.

When I was last at Hawarden this charm-

ing home of study was almost completed in its
arrangements. The shelves were crowded
with interesting books on theology, travel,
science, &c. In not a few of them one found
notes made by Mr. Gladstone, sometimes
queries, often additional remarks, which added
to their value. The choice of volumes was
made on no exclusive basis, and I noticed the
works of Churchmen, Catholics, and Noncon-
formists side by side. A certain proportion of
standard novels was also to be seen. Outside
the walls of the library there was provision
made for lawn-tennis, quoits, and croquet on
the spacious green sward, and these grounds,
I understood, were much appreciated by the
scholars of the intermediate school.

One of the last communications on a new
book from Mr. Gladstone, which was published
in the newspapers, was concerning a volume of
sermons by his old friend, the Rev. Dr. J.
Guinness Rogers. In the course of this letter,
he said, "As the day of parting draws nearer,
I rejoice to think how small the differences
between us have already become as compared
with the agreements." In connection with Mr.

Gladstone's book-collecting, his letter, written in September, 1896, to Mr. Bernard Quaritch is worth recalling.   In the course of this interesting piece of autobiography, Mr. Gladstone stated : " I have in my time been a purchaser to the extent of about thirty-five thousand volumes. A book-collector ought, as I conceive, to possess the following qualifications : —appetite, leisure, wealth, knowledge, discrimination, and perseverance. Of these I have only had two, the first and the last, and these are not the most important. Restricted visual power now imposes upon me a serious amount of disability ; and, speaking generally, I have retired from the list of purchasers."   Then, after reference to his foundation of St. Deiniol's Library, he continues : " The oldest book I have, that is to say, the one longest in my possession, was presented to me personally by Mrs. Hannah More. It is a copy of her ' Sacred Dramas,' printed and given to me in 1815. . . . My purchases commenced a few years after that time, and I have a variety of books acquired at Eton. Among them is a copy of Mr. Hallam's ' Constitutional History,' in

quarto, presented to me by his son Arthur, the
subject of 'In Memoriam,' and at that period
my dearest friend."

Mr. Gladstone concluded this statement as
to his work as a book-collector thus :—
"Though, as I have said, a beggarly collector,
I have had a few specialities. One I will
mention. I accumulated more than thirty
distinct *rifacciamenti* of the Book of Common
Prayer. Many of these had prefaces, which
commonly ran to this effect : ' The prayer-book
is excellent ; but it has some blemishes. Let
them be removed, and it will find universal
acceptance. Accordingly, I have performed
this operation ; and I now give the reformed
prayer-book to the world.' But I have never
obtained, and have never seen, a second edition
of any one of these productions. I greatly
doubt whether they have usually paid their
printer's bills. Book-collecting may have its
quirks and eccentricities ; but on the whole,
it is a vitalising element in a society honey-
combed by several sources of corruption. My
apology for the poor part I have played in it is
that it could only have the odds and ends, the

dregs and leavings of my time. And accordingly, I am aware that the report which I send you is a very meagre one. To mend it a little, I give to this pursuit in all its walks, from the highest (with which you are of all men the most conversant) downwards, my heartiest good wishes. And that I may not be ungrateful, I will apprise you that I still preserve among my most select possessions the beautiful copy on vellum of the Lyttelton-Gladstone translations which you were so good as to present to me."

Grand Old Bookman ! After such a delightful account by himself of his own interest in books, one regrets all the more that failing sight caused Mr. Gladstone to discontinue the autobiography which he had commenced. No other pen will be able to delineate so vividly and fully the acts and thoughts of one who experienced so long " the joy of eventful living."

CHAPTER VI.

A GUEST IN MANY HOMES.

MR. GLADSTONE was essentially "a citizen of the world," enjoying social intercourse with marvellous zest within a short time before he passed away. His memory of faces and facts aided him in conversation, and very rarely indeed did he fail to broach some topic on which those who met him in society were not interested.

One of the few occasions on which he made amusing mistakes in identity was at a dinner-party where Professor Stokes, President of the Royal Society, was a guest. Mr. Gladstone, who sat next to him, supposed him to be the Professor Stokes whose forte was Ecclesiastical History. So he plied him with questions as to various errors in the "History of the Irish Church." He turned at length to his silent companion, and inquired whether he did not agree with his views. "Well, sir, I really know nothing whatever about the subject," was the reply of Professor Stokes, of Cambridge. "But," said Mr. Gladstone, "you wrote the book." "No," said the Professor, "I certainly did not." "But," insisted Mr. Gladstone, "you are Professor Stokes." "Yes, that is true, but I am Professor of Physics at Cambridge, and therefore can hardly be regarded as an authority on ecclesiastical history!"

Mr. Gladstone and Mr. Bright were on another occasion at a party, where the famous French economist, M. Chevalier, was hoping to catch some words of wisdom from the lips of the two statesmen. But, by one of the perversities of fate, Mr. Gladstone and Mr. Bright did nothing but converse on corns and chiropody. This was all the more mysterious to the distinguished Frenchman, because he was under the impression that the discussion was on corn and the corn duties.

It reminds one of Tennyson's story of how, at his first meeting with Frederick W. Robertson, the nervous poet could talk of nothing but beer.

Another story, which is at all events *bien fondu,* is linked with a visit to Corton, the seat of Mr. J. J. Colman, head of the well-known mustard firm. It is said that Mr. Gladstone arrived rather late in the drawing-room one evening prior to dinner, and, advancing into the room, he rubbed his hands and asked quite innocently, "Well, are we all *mustered ?*" It was hardly possible for some of those present to refrain from smiling at this involuntary pun.

To see Mr. Gladstone at a dinner-party was always delightful; he seemed to enjoy so much the interchange of thought. The weight of the day's anxieties, the responsibilities of leading his party, the prospect of returning later in the evening to the House of Commons never affected his brilliant talk. When he was busiest, it was said that Mrs. Gladstone used to ask hostesses to place her by her husband's side at dinner-parties, in order that she might seize the rare opportunity of conversing with her husband ! Nothing certainly could exceed the old-fashioned courtesy he always showed to his wife; who accompanied him almost everywhere. When he visited Plymouth, some

I am very much concerned to hear that she is suffering from severe affliction which I am sure she will bear in a spirit the most likely to lead the way to comfort. Pray assure her to such if a proper opportunity arise. Yours very faithfully

W. E. Gladstone

EXTRACT FROM AN AUTOGRAPH LETTER FROM MR. GLADSTONE, RELATING
TO THE ILLNESS OF A DISTINGUISHED AUTHORESS.

years ago, the aged attached couple were much
amused to hear vendors of their portraits
shouting, " The Grand Old Man and his wife
—one penny !" Mrs. Gladstone shared the
interest felt in her husband ; and to sit next to
her was a delightful experience, for she was
ever ready to eulogise him.

I remember meeting Mrs. Gladstone once on
an afternoon when the result of a by-election
had just been announced. Immediately she
was informed of the Liberal victory which had
been won unexpectedly, she exclaimed, " Oh,
I must drive home immediately and tell
William !" She took the profoundest interest
in politics, though not a deep student of them,
just because of her husband's immersion in
them. She was always his companion on the
Midlothian campaigns and on the other
political tours which he took ; she it was who
prepared his refreshing cup of tea, infused for
just three minutes according to Sir Andrew
Clark's instructions ; and the famous egg-fillip
which sustained his voice through great
speeches was manufactured by her alone.

When the veteran couple were at a party in

recent years, it was quite pathetic to see how Mrs. Gladstone hovered around her distinguished husband. When he had been standing a long while, chatting to one and another, his hostess once begged him, in my hearing, to sit down and rest. "Oh, no, thank you," said Mr. Gladstone. "Ah," said the kindly lady, "you know Mrs. Gladstone would insist on it, if she were here." Immediately, with a smile, Mr. Gladstone sat down.

This was the picture drawn by a friendly hand of the way in which Mr. Gladstone spent his day, usually, when staying at a country house. "He was punctual at breakfast, and immediately after that meal retired to his own room, and was busily occupied with reading or writing till luncheon time. After luncheon he was ready for a walk or drive, a visit to any interesting object, or a friendly call. After a cup of tea at five o'clock he again retired to his room, and reappeared at dinner-time the gayest of the gay, full of fun and conversation, and prepared to bear his full share in the amusements of the evening, whether they took the form of

'Shakespeare and the musical glasses,' or a round game. At bedtime he disappeared, book in hand, and put in another hour or so of systematic reading before he lay down to sleep. He shone as a guest, being delightfully unspoilt, full of zest for common amusements, eager to please and be pleased, and curiously grateful for the least civility or attention."

Tennyson wrote in his diary in 1865 : "The great man, Gladstone, is coming to dine with us here [London] on Friday ; a compliment ; but how he can find time from the mighty press of business amazes me." When the Gladstones visited the Poet Laureate at Aldworth, the Haslemere home designed by their mutual friend, Mr. James Knowles, editor of *The Nineteenth Century*, this was one of the entries made by the Poet : "A very noble fellow, and perfectly unaffected. . . . Mr. and Mrs. Gladstone frisked about like boy and girl in the heather."

Mr. Gladstone was specially fond of spending a Sunday at the seat of his friends, the Leveson-Gowers, at Holmbury St. Mary, in

Surrey. James Russell Lowell was a fellow guest during the visit paid after the defeat of the Home Rule Bill, and thus wrote : "From Osterley I went to Holmbury (Leveson-Gower's), where I spent a couple of days very pleasantly with Mr. and Mrs. Gladstone and other guests. Mr. Gladstone was in boyish spirits. He told me among other things that 'in the whole course of his political experience he had never seen anything like the general enthusiasm of the country for Home Rule in Ireland.' I asked slyly 'if it was not possible that a part at least of this enthusiasm might be for the Prime Minister ?' 'Oh, no, not a bit of it !' he answered with eager emphasis. And I am inclined to think he believed it for a moment." What a light this sheds on the source of what was alike the strength and the weakness of the veteran statesman. As we read it now we are fain to adopt the saying of his successor over some other event, " we smile and pass on."

Another seat where Mr. Gladstone would frequently spend a week-end was Hatchlands, near Guildford, the home of Mr. Stuart (now

Lord) Rendel. Though situated at a convenient distance from London in case of emergency, it was yet sufficiently in the country to soothe and rest the wearied statesman. State affairs during Mr. Gladstone's Premierships were usually kept in abeyance during these little visits, though the writer can remember Mr. Arnold Morley once hurrying down from London and meeting Mr. Gladstone on his way home from church with a despatch-box containing an important paper for the right honourable gentleman's consideration. But this was quite the exception, for any intrusion upon Mr. Gladstone's Sabbatic rest was rare. He liked to walk in silence to the parish church, and in silence home again. In the church no worshipper was more attentive, no listener more eager to catch every word of the most commonplace discourse. On three or four occasions a foolish clergyman seized the opportunity of uttering a diatribe, in veiled language, against the policy of the statesman who was in his congregation. Such an incident only grieved Mr. Gladstone, who harboured no resentment against such an indiscreet preacher.

Wherever the Gladstones went as guests they
left pleasant memories. As Tennyson wrote
concerning their visit in 1871 : " One could
not but feel humbled in the presence of those
whose life was evidently one long self-sacrifice,
and, one would hope, quickened to more of it
in one's own life. Mrs. Gladstone wears
herself out by all her hospital work in
addition to the work of a Prime Minister's wife.
Her daughter helps her, and helps her brother
also in his bad Lambeth parish."

Mr. Gladstone was interested in all manner
of pursuits and recreations, although he had
strong views as to the evils of horse-racing,
which holds so prominent a place in the minds
of not a few politicians. Once upon a time,
he referred to the Derby Day as that
" mysterious Wednesday." With the thorough-
ness which has marked his every action through
life, the great statesman upon the occasion
of his visit to Epsom entered into the spirit of
the scene with terrible earnestness. His white
face was " the cynosure of every eye " as the
horses stood at the post on that eventful
afternoon that saw the downfall of the once

mighty Macgregor and the ridiculous antics of the absurd Cockney Boy.

He enjoyed especially his visit to the beautiful seat in Wales of the late Sir Hussey Vivian, who was raised to the peerage as Lord Swansea. On that occasion he was serenaded in the evening by a choir who sang delightfully some favourite airs and hymns.

It has been almost forgotten that Mr. Gladstone was once a guest of his great opponent, the Marquis of Salisbury, at Hatfield. "I can never think unkindly of Lord Salisbury," he used to remark, "since the day when I saw him as a little child in a red frock." When he went to Hatfield, Dr. Samuel Wilberforce was a fellow guest, and has left on record a pleasant account of the occasion. He describes Lord Salisbury and Mr. Gladstone walking about the park, and examining with interest the many fine trees, which must have offered a temptation to such a wielder of the axe as Mr. Gladstone used to be. Those who have been inside the stately home of Lord Salisbury may remember that on a table stands a carved model of the Grand Old Man with an axe.

In later years Mr. Gladstone was taken under the kindly wing of Mr. Armitstead, a former member for Dundee. In a happy pen portrait of this gentleman, whose figure became very familiar to the public in connection with the Gladstones, we read : "This tall stately Commoner even now is just the man to play the part of travelling host to such an illustrious pair. He might be some Viking who had escaped the ravages of time, and had been moulded and attired in the civilisation of our own age. His great height, long and flowing beard, passing from blonde to white, his keen fearless eyes, over-firm lips and curling moustache, constitute a *tout ensemble* which makes the wealthy Scotsman the 'Milor' of every Continental *garçon* and *cocher* and boulevard merchant. Mr. Armitstead speaks in strong yet kindly accents which acquit him the genial colossus that he is. If you ask of this interest in his famous guest, he will describe it as the proudest pleasure of his life, and say that he feels how deep is the compliment in Mr.

MRS. GLADSTONE AND MASTER WILLIAM GLADSTONE, THE HEIR.
(From a Photograph by G. W. WEBSTER, Chester.)

Gladstone in accepting from him the attentions which scores of people are always ready to give. . . . " I am an old man compared with Mr. Gladstone," he has sometimes said, " and he'll see all us weak old fellows into our graves." Nothing certainly could have exceeded the kindly provision made for his guests' comfort by Mr. Armitstead when they stayed at Blairgowrie, in Perthshire, and, in the autumn of 1897, at Butterstone House. When the weather was fine, the whole party would picnic out of doors, and these unconventional incidents were very agreeable to all. At such times Mr. Gladstone's spirits would be as high as those of the youngest member of the group, and few who saw him sitting on the heather bareheaded and in summer attire would have imagined that he had long passed his eightieth birthday. This visit to Dunkeld was destined to be the last of such experiences.

While writing of Mr. Gladstone as a guest in other homes, one must not omit to refer to his frequent visits to Dalmeny Park, the Edinburgh seat of the Earl of Rosebery, which was his headquarters during the memorable

Midlothian campaigns. In fulfilment of an old promise he stayed, a few years ago, at Malwood, the home of Sir William and Lady Vernon Harcourt in the New Forest. In many other houses he was a welcome guest, such as at Aston Clinton, where he was in sight of the Chiltern Hundreds, with which, in its technical sense, he was acquainted specially as a Parliamentarian. At Bowood, in the old days, and at Chatsworth, Mr. Gladstone was entertained on more than one occasion. He sought refreshment and change of air at Penmaenmawr, where his son Stephen gained better health after illness. When the Grand Old Man was at this little Welsh seaside resort, he used to fetch each morning the bread required for the household. It was the custom for visitors to call at the baker's for their loaves, as there was no cart to deliver them from door to door. Mr. Gladstone, not to be outdone, used to be seen walking hurriedly home with a large loaf under each arm.

CHAPTER VII.

LIFE AT HAWARDEN.

AFTER the consideration of Mr. Gladstone as a guest in other people's homes, one turns to his life in his own home. The Flintshire village of Hawarden had in the earlier part of the century, as we have mentioned, a somewhat ill repute. But in the last fifty years it has acquired a new fame as the residence of Mr. Gladstone.

In no way remarkable for picturesqueness, Hawarden would not attract the tourist, who visits the ancient city of Chester and Eaton Hall, the fine seat of the Duke of Westminster, were it not for its link with the life of the Gladstones. You may get to it from Chester easily by driving, or you may go by rail to either of two stations, whence Hawarden is not a long walk. There is the church of St.

Deiniol to be visited, the scene of so many occasions of interest to the pilgrim who is enthusiastic over Mr. Gladstone. The edifice stands in an ample churchyard, and its interior is kept with pious care. You cannot help turning your eyes to the reading-desk at which Mr. Gladstone stood so many times and read the lessons in that marvellous voice and style of his. Then you note the memorial to the late Mr. W. H. Gladstone, and another to a former matron of Mrs. Gladstone's Home. The rector has obviously High Church views, as you gather from more than one notice. There is evidently a reverent regard for the church and the solemnity of its services, judging by the requests as to the conduct of those who enter its sacred precincts. The assembling of crowds of non-worshippers, merely bent on seeing Mr. Gladstone, led to a strongly worded protest against the churchyard being thronged at the conclusion of the morning service on Sundays. Mr. Gladstone was inconvenienced often by the too pressing attentions of his admirers, and he used latterly to seek refuge in the Rectory after service. The richness of the Hawarden living has been largely exaggerated, for it is forgotten that four district churches, vicarages, and schools are connected with the parish church.

The Hawarden estate covers about four square miles. There are nearly 500 tenants. The castle was erected when the late Sir Stephen Glynne was a minor. The picturesque ivy-covered ruins of the old castle stand in the grounds. If you approach the castle from the road, the first noticeable part which will attract attention is the Golden Wedding porch. Entering it, you are soon in the old hall, and at the door of the dining-room. In this apartment, which looks out on the terraces, hang some fine family portraits. The library, or "Temple of Peace" as it is called, is full of mementoes of the career of Mr. Gladstone. Most people know the systematic arrangement of the room, with its well-filled shelves and its tables, devoted either to correspondence, to politics, or to literature. Outside this room, when I was at the castle, there were many walking-sticks, and quite a collection of axes, presented by various friends.

F

On the first floor upstairs one saw the organ at which the late Mr. W. H. Gladstone used to play. The simple appointments of Mr. Gladstone's bedroom were a reflection of the man's life. A few portraits of members of his family, and of one or two political friends—I fancy I saw a photo of Sir George Trevelyan among them—were hanging on the walls. The eye lighted on this illuminated text, "Thou wilt keep him in perfect peace whose mind is stayed on Thee," the keynote, surely, of that serene calm which characterised the greater portion of Mr. Gladstone's life.

In another room of Hawarden Castle I noticed an autographed portrait of Mr. A. J. Balfour, who has been on more than one occasion a guest of the family, and has the sincerest reverence for Mr. Gladstone.

What a succession of notable men and women have crossed the threshold of Hawarden Castle during the last half-century ! One thinks of the almost surreptitious visit of the late Charles Stewart Parnell ; of the constant visits of politicians of all shades of opinion ; of distinguished strangers like Li Hung Chang ; of the

Colonial Premiers who spent so memorable a time with Mr. Gladstone, the oldest living ex-Premier, last year ; the Armenian deputation and many others.

It was in May, 1897, that the Prince and Princess of Wales and Princess Victoria came to pay honour to Mr. and Mrs. Gladstone at Hawarden. They were staying at Eaton Hall, and the following account of their visit is interesting :—" Starting at half-past 11, after being photographed in front of the Hall, the Eaton house-party rode on the light railway running through the park to the Belgrave Lodge, where the Prince and Princess and suite and the Duke and Duchess alighted. Carriages were in attendance, and, preceded by outriders, the Duke drove the Princess of Wales, while the Prince and Princess Victoria, with the Duchess, the Duchess of Abercorn, and Capt. Holford and Miss Knollys followed in a wagonette. Hawarden Park was entered through what is known as the Bilberry Wood, and the Castle was reached shortly before one o'clock. The children and old women pensioners were drawn up in front of Mrs. Gladstone's

Home, and ranged in front of the Castle
entrance was a guard of honour of the 2nd
V.B.R.W.F., consisting of members of the
Hawarden, Flint, Caergwrle, Mold, and Holy-
well companies, under the command of
Colonel Davies Cooke, Major and Adjutant
Gough, Captains Hurlbutt and Keene, and
Lieutenant Leask. With this exception no
formality was observed, the visit being entirely of a private character. On the arrival
of the distinguished visitors the Volunteers
presented arms and the band struck up the
National Anthem.

"Mr. and Mrs. Gladstone and the members
of their family received their Royal Highnesses in the Golden Wedding porch, and
the meeting was of an extremely cordial
character, the Princess affectionately kissing
Mrs. Gladstone. There were also present the
Rev. Stephen and Mrs. Gladstone and children,
the Hon. Mrs. W. H. Gladstone and children,
Mr. and Mrs. Henry Gladstone, Mr. Herbert Gladstone, M.P., the Rev. Harry and
Mrs. Drew, Miss Helen Gladstone, and Miss
Wickham. After a few minutes had elapsed

MRS. GLADSTONE.
(*From a Photo by* VALENTINE, Dundee.)

the party came out of the library and proceeded to inspect the ruins of the Old Castle.
Mr. Gladstone gave his arm to the Princess of
Wales, and the Duke of Westminster followed
with Mrs. Gladstone, while the Prince walked
with Mr. Herbert Gladstone. The veteran
statesman briskly descended the steps from the
library, and he tackled the steep hill leading
to the interesting ruins in a manner delightful
to see, though, as he told the members of
the British Association in 1896, he seldom
essays the stiff climb now. Princess Victoria
was the only one of the visitors to enter the
Old Castle, the others being content with
viewing it from the exterior. On returning,
the Princess of Wales inspected with evident
interest four pretty black Pomeranian puppies
and their mother, the progeny of Mr. Gladstone's favourite dog. Two of the puppies,
named Gyp and Jummy, are very young,
and were in a small basket, and it is
probable the Princess will accept one of them.
During lunch the Buckley band discoursed a
selection of music on the Castle terrace, and
subsequently Mr. G. Watmough Webster, of

Chester, had the honour of photographing the Prince and Princess and Mr. and Mrs. Gladstone in the Golden Wedding porch. Mrs. Gladstone and the Prince were seated, and respectively behind them stood Mr. Gladstone and the Princess. The group, as may be readily imagined, was a striking one, and it will linger long in the recollection of those who were privileged to witness it.

"At 2.30 the distinguished party, amid the ringing cheers of the assembled villagers and others, and the playing by the Volunteer band of 'God save the Queen,' departed for Sandycroft Station, where their Royal Highnesses caught a special train for Euston. At the Castle the leave-taking was of a touching description. The Princess said, 'Good-bye, mother,' to Mrs. Gladstone, and the venerable lady stooping kissed Her Royal Highness on the cheek. Mr. and Mrs. Gladstone accompanied them to the station. Moor Lane, leading to the station, was lined with spectators, who demonstrated their loyalty by repeatedly and heartily cheering. At the station a guard of honour was formed by the Sandycroft Fire

Brigade.   The train moved off at 2.45 amid the loud cheering of the crowd assembled outside the station gates.   The Duke and Duchess returned to Eaton Hall, and Mr. and Mrs. Gladstone drove back to the Castle.".

A special importance attaches to the Muniment Room at Hawarden Castle.   It is four or five years, said *The Outlook*, since Mr. Gladstone built this adjunct to his Cheshire home, and in it is stored every single document of public and private interest which has passed through the veteran statesman's hands during his long and crowded career.   Every single letter he has received from the Queen, for instance, is there, and probably the whole of the papers affecting the Newcastle estates, of which he was the guardian.   The happy historian who is allowed to graze in these rich pastures will find everything in perfect order ; for what English statesman has ever been more scrupulous, even punctilious, than is Mr. Gladstone in all his public and private relations, and what public man has carried method more rigorously into all his doings ?

Tennyson, after his visit to Hawarden in

October, 1876, wrote :—" My dear Mrs. Gladstone, here we are returned to our winter quarters, which, however, we find at present colder than Aldworth. We retain golden memories of our visit to Hawarden, and your statesman, not like Diocletian among his cabbages, but among his oaks, axe in hand."

Nearly ten years ago there appeared an absolutely untruthful account of evictions on the Hawarden estate, a canard which had one good result in drawing forth a clear and valuable statement as to the matter. One tenant went so far as to characterise the reports as " thundering lies." Yet again and again was this account reprinted in newspapers opposed to the policy of Mr. Gladstone, despite the forcible and categorical contradictions given to it. When I visited Hawarden last, I found that the villagers held the family in the highest esteem. One saw portraits of the Grand Old Man and his wife in most cottages, and heard many touching stories of acts of kindness shown by every member of the family to tenants on the estate.

Sometimes Mr. Gladstone was present at the

audit dinner, given in the "Glynne Arms" Hotel, and he was always received by the company with the highest enthusiasm. His reminiscences and his thoughtful advice were greatly appreciated by the assembled farmers, and were of interest beyond the immediate circle to which the speech was addressed.

In the village the Hawarden Institute was a standing evidence of the family's solicitude for the welfare of the villagers, who, on their part, erected a fountain in memory of the Gladstone golden wedding, near the park gates. Many of the books in the library at the Institute have inscriptions from the pen of Mr. Gladstone. I noticed that the authorised Life by Mr. G. Barnett Smith, bore a characteristic, modest note in Mr. Gladstone's handwriting.

In one of his later speeches, the right hon. gentleman mentioned that one of the few public offices devolving upon him, which had not received his labours, was that of a county magistrate. His eldest son was elected unopposed to a seat on the County Council, and was a county magistrate. In not a few county enterprises, too, the Gladstones took their part.

Members of the family were interested in the
Mere Hey Colliery, and other commercial
ventures. And no good cause of philanthropy
initiated in the neighbourhood of Hawarden
has failed to receive generous assistance from
the inhabitants of the Castle."

CHAPTER VIII.

MR. GLADSTONE AS A CHURCHMAN.

ALLUSION has been already made to the decided attraction which theology always possessed for the subject of this biography. It was sometimes said that if Mr. Gladstone had not been Prime Minister he would have been Archbishop of Canterbury. But one could have prophesied quite as probably that he would have been Lord Chancellor or editor of *The Times*, for in whatsoever sphere he had chosen he would have become pre-eminent.

But he was undoubtedly a strong Churchman from his earliest days to the last year of his life, and was concerned deeply for the well-being of the Church of England. Only seven years ago he acquired the advowson and right of next presentation to the Rectory of Liverpool at a price which must have exceeded £10,000. The rector of Liverpool enjoys the patronage of three other churches in the city of Mr. Gladstone's birth : St. Matthias, Great Howard-street ; St. Matthew's, Scotland-road, and St. Stephen's, Byrom-street. The rector, too, is joint patron of three other livings, so his importance and influence is considerable. It was imagined that the Rev. Harry Drew would receive the presentation, but so far he remains at Buckley Vicarage.

Besides possessing the advowson of the rectory of Liverpool, Mr. Gladstone was patron of the incumbency of Seaforth Church and St. Thomas's, Toxteth. One of his early recollections was of visiting Cambridge with his father and mother, with the idea of his father obtaining from the venerable Mr. Simeon, leader of the Evangelical party, a nominee for the vicarage of Seaforth. Mr. Gladstone was a generous donor to Church funds, and gave quite recently £1,000 to the fund raised for relief of the poorer clergy. Together with the late Mr. Hope Scott ("the only man who could alone turn me round his little finger"), Mr. Gladstone founded Trinity College, Glenalmond, for training the Scotch Episcopal clergy.

Photo by]

A PICNIC AT BLACKCRAIG, SEPTEMBER 16, 1893.

[VALENTINE, Dundee.

When the jubilee of the college came round, he gave most interesting reminiscences of its early days.

Many years ago he was a prominent figure at various Church gatherings. He took part in the farewell to the noble Bishop Selwyn. In the St. Asaph diocesan assemblies he was an occasional visitor, and once read a paper. In all the ecclesiastical struggles—the Gorham question, the censure of Professor Maurice, the prosecution of Archdeacon Denison, &c.—he was an interested participant. Nearly forty years ago he spoke at a meeting in aid of the Central African Mission, attended by Dr. Livingstone. In 1855 Bishop Wilberforce recorded in his diary: "Easter Day. To Chapel Royal. I preached with interest. Gladstone amongst others, to whom went afterwards and had a talk. Noble as ever. His sympathies with Conservatives, his opinions with Liberals. No good to the Church to come from Parliament. It must be developed from within. He would not go on in politics to the end on any consideration." The last sentence has a peculiar importance.

His regular church-going was noted from an early period in his career as a public man. One Maundy Thursday evening, coming out of All Saints', Margaret-street, Mr. Tom Collins remarked to Sir Stafford Northcote, "One would think no politician ever said his prayers but W. E. G., so absurd is the publicity which attends his devotions." When in London he often went to the services at the Chapel Royal, and just before his resignation he might have been seen listening to the Bishop of Ripon in that attitude so familiar to members of the House of Commons—his hand curved to make an ear-trumpet, his head well forward, and every feature of the noble face alert. When the congregation sang as a parting hymn—

> O Paradise, O Paradise !
> Who does not long for rest ?

one could hardly resist the application of the words to the venerable statesman, who was joining heartily in the singing.

One must mention especially in this chapter the admirable exercise of Church patronage which distinguished Mr. Gladstone's years of office. The majority of his appointments to bishoprics have now lapsed by death and resignation. Most of the men he chose were High Churchmen, but nearly all of them were of high ability, and obtained conspicuous success. His letters offering, on behalf of the Crown, the various Sees were gems of epistolary discretion. He was less concerned with the politics of the recipients than with their qualifications, and his choice was again and again verified by the result.

While writing of Mr. Gladstone as a Churchman, one must not forget to complete the record by saying that he had a broad and tolerant sympathy with all, whether in the Church of England or in other communions, who were serving their Master. And this was evidenced on several occasions when he wrote or spoke kind words to various leaders in the Free Churches. He was the guest of Dr. Guinness Rogers and of Dr. Joseph Parker, to name only two of these leaders, and had a wide knowledge of most of the distinguished Nonconformist preachers and writers of the day. With Mr. Spurgeon he corresponded on more than one occasion, and he attended the Metro-

politan Tabernacle at least once when that
eminent man preached.

The secret of this broad sympathy was revealed in Mr. Gladstone's love of earnestness.
Canon Knox-Little said, not long ago, in Man-
chester Cathedral, that it was a diabolical lie
to say that religion was outside common life,
and illustrated his remark by Mr. Gladstone's
career, adding : "A religious man ought first
of all to be in earnest. He remembered that
dear and good man, over whose sorrows and
weakness and suffering the whole country,
without distinction of party, was watching and
thinking at Hawarden Castle, saying to him,
' You may make mistakes, but whether you do,
do it as if it were the one thing to be done.'
In other words, that was 'Be in earnest.'"

CHAPTER IX.

MR. GLADSTONE'S FRIENDS.

SIDELIGHTS of a valuable kind are thrown on every man's character by his choice of friends. Mr. Gladstone was no exception to this rule.

Though a politician, it may be admitted at once that he did not select his friends because of their political opinions; and, unless a colleague had more than mere political sympathies to recommend him, he was not admitted to Mr. Gladstone's circle of friends. Yet, as he was thrown into close contact with members of his own party, it was natural that many of them became his intimates.

His early friends—Doyle, Hope Scott, Lyttelton, and others—have been already mentioned in these pages. It remains to allude to the men who in later years were the friends of Mr. Gladstone. The names of several occur

G

to the mind at once. There was Lord Acton, one of the wisest men in Europe, whose erudite knowledge of history, ecclesiastical and political, was a continual delight to Mr. Gladstone. He once persuaded this Catholic peer to accept a Court appointment, although Lord Acton was much more at home in a library than at a Levee. On the visits to the Continent which Mr. Gladstone paid so frequently, Lord Acton was a welcome companion, for he had as great an interest in the antiquarian treasures stored in famous museums as his aged friend. There were few subjects on which the two men could not discourse with interest, and none on which they could not utter words well worth remembering.

Another friend was Mr. John Morley, whose position as a critic and historian was less assailable than his reputation as a statesman. Mr. Morley's convictions on the Irish Question were, undoubtedly, a great support to Mr. Gladstone, and his intellectual ability, added to the regard and veneration which he felt for his leader, made him specially welcome at Hawarden, and in any house where the

Gladstones were residing. Perhaps some day it will be shown that in Mr. Morley's religious attitude there was much more sympathy with that of Mr. Gladstone than was imagined. They were similar, at all events, in sincere pity for misfortune and misery, and the pitiable condition of the Irish peasant had a good deal to do with their firm belief in Home Rule as a panacea for certain ills. Mr. Morley's supposed coldness vanished immediately in the cordial atmosphere of the Gladstone family, and no member of the party enjoyed more keenly the pleasures of a walk and a talk with Mr. Gladstone.

The kindly care exercised by Lord Rendel and Mr. Armitstead over the veteran statesman has been described. No two friends of Mr. Gladstone were quite so dissimilar in temperament as the English peer and the stalwart Scot. Lord Rendel's charming château, the Villa Thorenc, at Cannes, came to be regarded as the South of France home of Mr. Gladstone. There he guarded the Grand Old Man from the inquisitiveness of hero-worshippers; there he arranged all sorts of pleasant excursions for his

distinguished guests.   Not a Welshman by
birth, Lord Rendel won Montgomeryshire in
1880 from the Conservatives, who had regarded
it as one of the safest seats in the Principality.
From that period may be said to date his close
friendship with Mr. Gladstone, who was ever
mindful of such services to the cause.   The
intimate relations between the two families was
further cemented by the marriage of Miss
Maud Rendel to Mr. H. N. Gladstone.   Lord
Rendel once said, "A day with Mr. Gladstone
is a liberal education," and certainly he was an
authority on the subject.   When Mr. Gladstone formed his last Cabinet it was in his
friend's town house that the historic *pourparlers*
took place.   Lord Rendel always took Mr.
Gladstone's age seriously, and no one could
have cared more assiduously for him than the
trim, grey-haired peer, who, for his many
services to the Grand Old Man, won the thanks
of all the latter's friends.

Sir Donald Currie must not be forgotten, for
his delightful sea-voyages did much to restore
Mr. Gladstone's health after severe strains
upon it.   In June, 1895, Mr. and Mrs. Glad-

stone were the guests of Sir Donald Currie on board the *Tantallon Castle*, and had an opportunity of witnessing the opening of the Baltic Canal. On June 13, the steamer arrived in the Elbe, and the visitors went to Hamburg. At a dinner on board the *Tantallon Castle*, the burgomaster proposed the health of the ex-Premier, alluding to him as " The Right Reverend" ! Some of Sir Donald's guests took the opportunity of visiting Friedrichsruhe, the seat of Prince Bismarck. If Mr. Gladstone had met the ex-Chancellor, the occasion would have been particularly interesting. When the vessel was at Copenhagen, the King and Queen of Denmark, with other members of the Royal family, came on board to luncheon. The King proposed the health of Mr. Gladstone, who, in reply, proposed the Queen's health, alluding in flattering terms to the Princess of Wales. Afterwards the Royal party were photographed on board.

On a previous voyage under Sir Donald Currie's auspices, the Gladstones were fellow-guests with Tennyson, who was sounded as to whether he would accept a peerage. During this sea trip the late Tsar of Russia came on board with other exalted personages, and the Poet Laureate was persuaded to read some of his poems aloud. Of course, " Maud " was one of the selected pieces, and a humorous story was circulated that Tennyson, quite abstractedly held an exalted Royal lady's hand during the reading, and gave it gentle pressure at certain sentimental passages !

Mr. Gladstone and the Poet Laureate were old friends, as has been made evident in the charming " Life of Tennyson " issued recently by his son. The biographer gives more than one valuable and new dictum of Mr. Gladstone ; for instance, concerning politics, the present Lord Tennyson writes : " At one time he consulted Mr. Gladstone as to my taking up a political life. Mr. Gladstone wrote in answer that my father must recollect that a political life was 'surrounded by an adamantine wall,' that a man in politics was apt to ' lose the finer moral sense,' and that the political outlook ahead was ' full of storms.' "

It is time some allusion were made to Lady Frederick Cavendish, who is fully entitled to

be considered one of Mr. Gladstone's friends.
As his niece she was always a favourite visitor,
and after her marriage to the brother of the
present Duke of Devonshire she was doubly
allied with one who was her husband's political
leader. When Lord Frederick Cavendish
was assassinated under such tragic circumstances in Phœnix Park, at the opening of
his career as Irish Secretary, the bereaved
widow turned to Mr. and Mrs. Gladstone for
consolation. Lady Frederick, though she felt
her terrible loss acutely, was able to say to
Mr. Gladstone through her tears, "Uncle
William, you did right to send him." She
gave herself to philanthropic work with
renewed ardour, and found her solace in
alleviating the sorrows of others. Of Lady
Frederick Mr. Gladstone once said, "She is
one of the holiest women I ever knew."

Mr. Gladstone kept his friendships in good
repair by adding to the inner circle of his
intimates young recruits. Among these must
be named Mr. George W. E. Russell, who was
enabled by his thorough acquaintance with Mr.
Gladstone to write the best biography of him

which has yet appeared. Mr. Russell was quite *au fait* in all matters Gladstonian, and to his pen we owe many interesting pictures of the Grand Old Man. He was a frequent visitor to Hawarden, and was often invited to the same house-parties as those attended by Mr. Gladstone.

One must certainly include Mr. Gladstone's private secretaries in this account of his friends, for they stood in a specially familiar and pleasant relationship to their chief. In 1894 Mr. Gladstone dined with various gentlemen who acted in close official connection with him during his four Premierships. In the company which assembled at Brooks's Club were Sir Reginald E. Welby, Sir Arthur Godley, Sir Algernon West, Sir R. H. Meade, Sir James Carmichael, M.P., Mr. E. W. Hamilton, Mr. H. W. Primrose, Mr. Leveson-Gower, M.P., Mr. Horace Seymour, Mr. Spencer Lyttelton, Mr. G. H. Murray, and Mr. Shand. When he left office, Mr. Gladstone recommended the bestowal of a peerage on Sir Reginald Welby, Sir Algernon West became a Privy Councillor, and Commanderships of the

Bath were conferred on Mr. Spencer Lyttelton and Mr. G. H. Murray. Other honours had been already given to former secretaries, so that it will be seen that Mr. Gladstone was not unmindful of those who served him so faithfully. In the days of his Premierships it was said that 30,000 letters used to be received by Mr. Gladstone every year, of which, of course, the greater number by far were answered by his secretaries. They knew to a nicety which portion of this huge correspondence must be undertaken by the Prime Minister himself, and which should be spared from his already over-busy pen. In his last administration Sir Algernon West was of immense value to Mr. Gladstone, who was delighted to avail himself of his skilful and discreet aid.

The late Sir Andrew Clark stood in the relation of friend to his renowned patient quite as much as of physician. From the day when the young doctor first attracted Mrs. Gladstone's attention at the London Hospital, Andrew Clark was a valued and esteemed acquaintance of all the Gladstone family. It was a strange commentary on the uncertainty of life that it

fell to the sad lot of Mr. Gladstone to act as
pall-bearer at his physician's funeral, although
Sir Andrew was seventeen years younger. It
was in order to speak at the meeting called
to commemorate Sir Andrew Clark that Mr.
Gladstone braved a slight attack of illness, and
his fine eulogy of his late physician was
actually the last speech delivered by him in
London. In this connection it is worth while
recalling some of the words used by Sir
Andrew about his celebrated patient. "Mr.
Gladstone," said the physician, "is a man of
marvellous physical as well as mental endow-
ments, and, notwithstanding his advanced
years, he has in many respects still all the
freshness, elasticity, and vigour of youth. His
muscular and arterial systems are both extra-
ordinarily well preserved, and the force, energy,
and versatility of his nervous powers are far
beyond those of an ordinary man in the prime
of life. . . . Even after the rejection of the
Home Rule Bill, and the great crisis which
followed, Mr. Gladstone's sleep was unim-
paired, and his physical condition uninjured.
To Mr. Gladstone work is not exhausting, but

is restorative." It was mentioned in the life of Bishop Harold Browne that when Sir Andrew Clark examined him in the summer of 1884 he declared that he knew but one other man of his years with so sound a constitution. That other man was Mr. Gladstone, and Sir Andrew added, "I cannot see the chink through which his soul will escape."

Another life-long friend of Mr. Gladstone was Sir Henry Acland, whose profound knowledge and charming character were always his admiration. Dr. Ginsburg may be termed also a friend; his scholarly labours found in Mr. Gladstone a constant appreciator. Many other names will occur of those who were closely connected with the right honourable gentleman during his long career, and they would all testify to the uniform courtesy and generosity which distinguished the friendship of Mr. Gladstone.

CHAPTER X.

HIS INTEREST IN PHILANTHROPY.

FROM his earliest days Mr. Gladstone took a
deep interest in various charitable societies, to
which, indeed, he was a far more generous
donor than the general public was aware. He
was very careful, as was also Mrs. Gladstone,
in the bestowal of influence and money. But
when once he felt assured of the excellence of
any work, he never relinquished his support
of it.

For his knowledge of philanthropic societies
he depended mostly on his wife. In the East-
end to this day, though it is a generation ago,
the whole-hearted labours of Mrs. Gladstone
during the cholera epidemic are remembered
gratefully by the poor. She had, previous to
this, been a regular visitor at the London
Hospital, whose wards were filled in 1866 with

the sick and the dying, on account of this epidemic. Many of the parents left orphans ; these Mrs. Gladstone would often convey to her own house, or to a house at Clapton which she had taken for the purpose. She roused the interest of her friends, and obtained clothes for those who had lost their all. Then, needing more money than she could provide herself, Mrs. Gladstone wrote a touching letter to *The Times*, with the result that £5,000 was subscribed quickly in aid of the orphans.

Having seen the constant deaths which ensued from want of care during convalescence, Mrs. Gladstone established the convalescent home at Woodford which bears her name. She has never ceased to take a strong personal interest in the conduct of the home ; many of those who benefited by it were selected by her from the patients whom she visited every Monday morning at the London Hospital.

Close to Hawarden Castle stands an Orphanage for Boys, whose origin dates back to the cotton famine in Lancashire which followed the American War in 1862. A large

number of men who were out of work in
Lancashire were brought to Hawarden, and
employed in making footpaths in the park.
Some of the men's daughters came at the same
time, and were housed in a convenient
mansion which had been the dower-house of
the former occupants of Hawarden.   It may
be mentioned, in passing, that then the Castle
was called Broad Lane Hall. Mrs. Gladstone
organised a regular training-home for these
girls, and afterwards found places for them as
domestic servants, although the majority of
them had been previously mill-hands. At the
present time this house, which has had such
curious changes during its history, is used as
an orphanage for working lads.

Not long ago, I had the pleasure of visiting
the Home, and saw a number of healthy boys
at dinner. The matron gave me some interesting particulars of the success which had
attended this Home. The careers of its
inmates are carefully recorded, and it was
pleasant to hear that at least one lad, after
leaving the orphanage, had sent a good con-
tribution to its funds. The boys go out

during the day to work in gardens, and on farms, returning to the Home at night. Near to the Castle, also, stands a dwelling-place for a few old ladies who, having come to poverty, are here cared for to the end of their days. So youth and old age are together the objects of generous thought by the Gladstones.

Mrs. Gladstone was one of the first to aid the penitentiary work carried on at Clewer. An incident in connection with this led to one of the very few occasions when Mr. Gladstone appeared in a law court. He prosecuted a man who attempted to blackmail him early in his Parliamentary life.

Another philanthropy in which the Gladstones were interested was the House of Charity, in Soho. The Salvation Army had warm supporters in various members of the family, and General Booth's interview with Mr. Gladstone at Hawarden will be remembered. Allusion was made on another page to the sympathy shown to the Newport Market Refuge by Mr. and Mrs. Gladstone.

An example of the personal philanthropy of Mr. Gladstone was recorded some years ago, when a clergyman, who had often noticed a crossing-sweeper near Harley-street, missing him from his accustomed place, visited the man in his wretched home. He found him ill and unable to leave his bed, and, having asked him if any of the clergy had visited him, the the crossing-sweeper replied, " Well, no, sir; no one has come except Mr. Gladstone ; he comes and reads and prays with me."

CHAPTER XI.

EPISODES IN AN EVENTFUL LIFE.

DURING the last thirty years especially there were many momentous incidents in Mr. Gladstone's career. There was, for instance, the great meeting held on Blackheath Common in 1871. He had been taunted with inattention to his Greenwich constituents, many of whom had suffered by the reduction of Dockyard establishments. Conservatives dared him to show his face in the neighbourhood ; Liberals declared it would be unwise, impolitic, and dangerous to risk a visit, considering the excited and hostile state of public opinion. Mr. Gladstone, entirely unmoved by either reasons, announced that he would be glad to meet his constituents (literally, in the open) on a Saturday afternoon, so that the working classes

H

might attend. The vast area of Blackheath Common was selected for this demonstration of Mr. Gladstone's courage.

Accompanied by his wife, he drove up in an open carriage punctually to the time, and saw a marvellous sight. Between fifteen and twenty thousand people stood in serried ranks, ready to howl at, and even injure, their member. Mr. Gladstone rose and, bare-headed, faced the great throng. For several minutes angry shouts from thousands made his voice inaudible. At length the patient determination and quiet dignity of the man caused silence. Then, as by the wand of a magician, one of the most extraordinary victories was won by straightforwardness and eloquence. The silence, as the speaker proceeded, became breathless, despite the discomfort of the huge crowd which swayed in front of the platform, and stretched far into the distance. In the waning light of the October afternoon, Mr. Gladstone consummated his personal triumph by a grand peroration. Then those who had come to insult and assault him rushed forward with a common impulse, and surrounded the orator with hands eager to clasp his. The air rang with cheers for Mr. and Mrs. Gladstone, and what had been prophesied would be a fiasco proved a magnificent success.

The seven Midlothian campaigns, each so different in its results, but each so similar in its enthusiasm, cannot be omitted from this chapter. The extraordinary physique of Mr. Gladstone was proved during the first of these campaigns, when he addressed 75,000 people within a fortnight. Who that was present can ever forget the great gatherings, some presided over by the veteran Sir John Cowan, of Beeslack, some by the Earl of Rosebery, then beginning his political career? Who could forget the torchlight processions which escorted Mr. Gladstone home after his great efforts? How the world watched his brilliant personality during those historic scenes, and marvelled at his versatility, adroit appeals to popular sentiment, solemn denunciations of his opponents' policy, and humorous sallies at their expense!

These were the occasions when he popularised those "railway-station speeches," which were the occasion of so much enthusiasm and also criticism. In most cases, it seemed that at whatsoever place Mr. Gladstone halted his party gained victories. In the midst of his first Midlothian campaign he interpolated a very fine address as Lord Rector of Glasgow University. He concluded with these words to the students :—" Be thorough in all you do, and remember that though ignorance often may be innocent, pretension is always despicable. Be you, like men, strong, and the exercise of your strength to-day will give you more strength to-morrow. Work onwards and work upwards, and may the blessing of the Most High soothe your cares, clear your vision, and crown your labours with reward."

The fine series of speeches which Mr. Gladstone delivered in connection with the Bradlaugh controversy deserve mention. I shall not forget the dignified speech in which he supported the motion for expunging the resolutions of expulsion of Mr. Bradlaugh when the latter lay dying in 1891. The speech in which he introduced his last Reform Bill, in 1884, must also be noted. Following this, in order

MR. GLADSTONE IN HIS LAST PREMIERSHIP

(From a Photo by BARRAUDS.)

of date, was his brilliant oration in 1886, when he placed before the House of Commons his Home Rule Bill.   No one, however much they differed from the opinions of Mr. Gladstone could withhold admiration from the lucid and eloquent manner in which the veteran Premier strove to persuade Parliament to meet the Irish demands.

The celebration of Mr. and Mrs. Gladstone's golden wedding in July, 1889, was very interesting, as it enabled Mr. Gladstone's opponents, as well as his friends, to unite in tributes. A great reception was given to the venerable couple at the National Liberal Club, at which thousands were present. In the village of Hawarden a drinking fountain was erected, and the family built a handsome porch to the Castle in honour of this happy jubilee of married life.

In December, 1892, Mr. Gladstone was the recipient of the freedom of the city of Liverpool, and delivered a charming speech in St. George's Hall.

When Mr. Gladstone introduced his second Home Rule Bill in 1893, he attained another oratorical success. For two hours and a quarter

he unfolded to a brilliant assembly the prin-
ciples of his measure. The Prince of Wales,
the Duke of York, many Ambassadors, Peers,
peeresses, and distinguished men of all parties
sat entranced while the Old Man Eloquent proceeded step by step through the complexities
of the Bill. These were the impressive words
with which he concluded: "It would be a
misery to me if I had omitted, in these closing
years, any measure possible for me to make
towards upholding and promoting the cause
which I believe to be the cause not of one
party or another, one nation or another, but of
all parties and all nations inhabiting these
islands. To those nations, viewing them as I
do, with all their vast opportunities, under a
living union for power and for happiness; to
those nations I say, let me entreat you, and if
it were my latest breath, I would entreat you
to let the dead bury its dead, to cast behind
you every recollection of bygone evils, and to
cherish, to love, to sustain one another through
all the vicissitudes of human affairs in the times
that are to come."

No wonder, after such a feat of ability and

endurance, Oliver Wendell Holmes should
have written :—

Think not the date a worn-out king assigned
As Life's full measure holds for all mankind ;
Shall Gladstone, crowned with eighty years, withdraw ?

Yet the sands of his political career were
running out swiftly, and early in 1894 it was
rumoured that Mr. Gladstone intended to resign
the Premiership and retire from Parliament.
Though guarded contradictions were published,
the report was justified when Mr. Gladstone
went to Windsor, accompanied by his wife, on
Friday, March 2, on a visit to the Queen. On
Saturday the Queen held a Council, attended
by Mr. Gladstone, the Earl of Kimberley, Earl
Spencer, the Marquis of Ripon, and Sir William
Harcourt, after which Mr. Gladstone resigned
office. It was all so sudden that people realised
with difficulty that his speech accepting the
Lords' amendments to the Local Government
Bill was actually the last he would ever deliver in
the Senate of which he was the chief ornament.
Thus he realised at last the hope he had
expressed five years before, when in writing to
Lord Tennyson he had said :—" Wish for me,
I pray you, a speedy deliverance, if God's will

may so be, from the life of turmoil and conten-
tion which I have pursued for fifty-seven years
and part of a fifty-eighth."

A touching incident occurred on the day when
Lord Rosebery kissed hands on his appointment as Prime Minister. The new Premier had
scarcely left the gates of Buckingham Palace
when Mr. Gladstone was seen driving past with
his daughter, Mrs. Drew, and his granddaughter
Dorothy. The crowd hailed the old warrior put-
ting off his armour with even greater enthusiasm
than it had just accorded his successor.

Mr. Gladstone's two speeches on the Armenian
atrocities, at Chester and Liverpool respectively, claim notice. They were full of that holy
passion for righteousness which transforms the
most ordinary sentences into rhetoric. These
two proved his last public utterances, and they
are a fine conclusion to the thousands of
speeches delivered by him.

The bows of eloquence are buried with the
archers, but let us hope that many a successor
to William Ewart Gladstone, with soul as
sincere and voice as thrilling, will arise in the
days that are to come.

CHAPTER XII.

AN APPRECIATION.

IT were easier, and perhaps wiser, to use the
words of others in a final tribute to Mr.
Gladstone's complex and interesting personality. One cannot hope to paint a more
delightful portrait of the orator, for instance,
than is revealed in Tennyson's lines :—

> Great ! for he spoke and the people heard,
>   And his eloquence caught like a flame
> From year to year of the world, till his word
>   Had won him a noble name.

The Poet Laureate also put on record this
opinion of his friend, from the politician's
standpoint. In a letter to Mr. Gladstone he
said, " Care not, you have done great work, and,
if even now [1874] you rested, your name
would be read in one of the fairest pages of
English history. I say this, however much on
some points of policy we may have differed."

Another discriminating critique was written by the late Lord Selborne, who in later years opposed Mr. Gladstone's policy. He said in a letter to a leading politician : "Gladstone, with all these qualities which make one admire and love him, baffles all calculation by the great individuality of his mind ; at once conscientious and ambitious, subtle and vehement, impulsive and discriminating. He is a comet, the elements of whose orbit are as yet but imperfectly known."

The Marquis of Salisbury spoke of his great rival as " one of the most brilliant figures who had served the State since Parliamentary Government in this country began," and alluded to Mr. Gladstone's " resolution, and the courage and the self-discipline which he had exhibited down to the latest period of the longest life ever granted to any English public statesman." To these judgments on Mr. Gladstone as a politician one needs to add no words. It only remains for the writer to strive to summarise the qualities which distinguished the man, as apart from the statesman.

First and foremost, one must take into

account the deep religiousness of Mr. Gladstone. It was this which sustained him in the
most anxious times; it was this which soothed
and calmed his latest days. In the speech
which he delivered in memory of his physician,
he sketched involuntarily one of his own
leading characteristics. It was the sentence in
which he spoke of the "profound sense of
religion which attended him through his whole
life, which supplied him with its guiding
principle, and which produced in him this
singular result, that when his mind had been
occupied and absorbed in the arduous questions continually brought before him, it was
his delight—and all those who knew him will,
I am quite sure, sustain me in what I say—
it was his delight and practice to find recreation not in frivolities, but in betaking himself naturally to the consideration of divine
things."

Other qualities which distinguished him
were fearlessness and pertinacity. Once
convinced of the righteousness of a cause,
he strove with indomitable courage to
promote its success. The Duke of Devonshire

described him as "throwing himself into
political conflict with double the ardour of
men of not half his years, and performing
feats not only of mental, but of physical vigour,
which might put younger men to the blush."
The same earnestness he displayed in literary
labours. Lord Rosebery—to call another
witness—spoke of him "as a learner and as a
reader, ever with his books, ever among his
books ; ever trying to learn something, as if
he had half a century before him in which
to work—nay, but truly as if he had eternity
before him in which to work."

Then, one must not forget his courtesy, so
particularly charming and so freely accorded
to all who met him. Search through all the
volumes of biography published during the
last half-century, and one is bold enough to
claim that you will not find an instance of
Mr. Gladstone's discourtesy, even in the face
of virulent denunciation and unmanly rudeness
on the part of others. He had a soul too
great for such ignoble slights, and throughout
his long public life there is hardly a case of an
unkind phrase in his reported utterances.

"APE'S" FIRST CARTOON OF MR. GLADSTONE, IN 1869.

(*Reproduced by kind permission from "Vanity Fair."*)

"Great empires and little minds go ill together," and assuredly Mr. Gladstone was not one of those

> Who for the poor renown of being smart,
> Would leave a sting within a brother's breast.

His vital interest in everybody and everything must be mentioned. It was this which elevated him into an importance and fame far exceeding that of a statesmen. Of course, his volume of ideas was occasonally disconcerting. A Cabinet colleague pictured him, more than thirty years ago, coming to the Cabinet charged to the muzzle with all sorts of schemes and all sorts of reforms which were absolutely necessary in his opinion to be undertaken immediately. Lord Palmerston used to look fixedly at the paper before him, saying nothing until there was a lull in Mr. Gladstone's outpouring. He then tapped the table, and said cheerfully, "Now, my lords and gentlemen, let us go to business!"

The ease with which he dismissed subjects from his mind, and turned for recreation to other themes, was marvellous. Not less extraordinary was his ability to rest. Hardly ever in his exciting career did he lose his sleep. All this pointed to immense will power, which sustained him in most difficult crises. He willed to live, and this eagerness for life was a valuable aid to his health. Mrs. Gladstone told the writer that her husband was once standing near an open window, through which came the shrill tones of a passing newsboy, shouting, "Death of Mr. Gladstone ! Speshul !" The right honourable gentleman turned quietly to one of the company who had heard it, and remarked, "Not just yet."

He was very patient, though many might doubt it. Those who saw Mr. Gladstone waiting hour after hour on the Treasury bench, listening to the dullest and dreariest speakers with interest, will, however, acknowledge his possession of this rare quality ; and he had humility, a sister virtue. Davenant said—

Your politicians
Have evermore a taint of vanity ;

and one would not deny that Mr. Gladstone appreciated thoroughly the popularity which came to him in later years. He enjoyed, as who would not ? the enthusiasm which greeted his appearances in public, and the love and honour rendered to him in private life. But from vanity he was free. The interest which crowds took in him was always something of a mystery to him, although it was pleasant to be regarded in so kindly a fashion.

And lastly, in this brief review of Mr. Gladstone's character, one may place one of his finest qualities—his faith. For him, though *VIII* acute suffering came to bear him company as "a final lesson—a final trial," there was ever present a radiant hope. No clouds of pain were allowed to obscure the sun of his enduring faith. It was not only faith in a future life, it was faith in the certainty of victory for true righteousness and real progress. He believed in "the pure might of good," and in that faith his whole career was lived.

CHAPTER XIII.

FROM WEARINESS TO REST.

It was in the early dawn of Ascension Day, 1898, that Mr. Gladstone laid down the burden of his long life. No other day in the whole year was more appropriate for the death of one who was the greatest son of the Church whom this century has seen ; no other day was more fitting for the final flight of the weary soul which was longing for release.

I have never seen Hawarden looking fairer than on the last day of Mr. Gladstone's life. Passing through the single street of the village, I entered the park, and was soon gazing at the windows of the room in which the sufferer was taking his leave of the world. After the night's rain, all the vari-coloured foliage around the castle was glistening in warm sunshine. The giant elms and cedars, the chestnut trees and oaks, seemed to guard as sentinels the historic home of the Gladstones. Rooks flew in ceaseless activity from tree to tree, and their caws filled the morning air. On the terrace, where so often Mr. Gladstone had welcomed crowds of visitors from far and wide, I saw proud peacocks strutting, the sunshine falling upon their gay plumage and giving it a dazzling radiance. Away in the distance the hills were covered with a slight mist, which revealed more glories of landscape as the day wore on.

The room in which the warrior was fighting with that last conqueror of all, was a different one from the chamber which he usually occupied. It had a southern aspect, and was on the first floor upstairs. Before the patient had been removed to it a partition in it had been taken down, so that there was plenty of space for the members of the family, as well as the doctors and nurses in attendance. A couch was also placed in the room, so that Mrs. Gladstone was able occasionally to rest from her sad vigil.

I

I learned from one of the physicians that beyond a Japanese screen and a few chairs there
was little furniture in the apartment. On its
walls were some portraits of Mr. Gladstone's
loved ones and friends. He lay on a low bed-
stead, his back to the light which streamed from
the window and told of the lovely weather outside. Beneath his windows the gardeners were
mowing the lawns, and one could not help
thinking of that " Reaper whose name is
Death," whose scythe was soon to remove the
most illustrious Englishman of the day.

On the previous night—May 17—it had been
thought improbable that Mr. Gladstone would
survive. Mr. Henry Gladstone, the eldest son,
had hurried by special train from London, and
the Rev. Stephen Gladstone had returned from
Colwyn Bay; while Dr. Habershon had hastened
through the night to his famous patient's
bedside. In a room in the Boys' Orphanage,
near to the castle, the anxious representatives of
the press had waited through the leaden hours,
and the village post-office had remained open to
transmit the bulletins which were posted every

few hours in the porch. It was pathetic to think of the aged partner of Mr. Gladstone's life and her sons and daughters in that upper room, watching the laboured breathing and signs of the coming change in the dying man. At four o'clock it was seemingly impossible for Mr. Gladstone to have rallied, but his wonderful vitality again enabled him to wrestle and conquer. Then at last some of the family retired to rest, and the news that the sufferer was in a gentle slumber brought relief to the watchers.

All the next day — May 18 — there was alternate rally and relapse, but the end came nearer and nearer. Mr. Gladstone muttered a word or two during the reading of hymns and prayers, as if he recognised the old familiar words, and once he said " Amen " in quite strong tones. To the hymn of his life—so musical, so fraught with blessing to many—was fast approaching its Amen, and one hardly dared to hope for a delay. Scores of kindly messages came from all parts of the world, and the telegraph messengers made a continual pro-

cession to and from the castle. The Queen and
the Prince of Wales sent affectionate inquiries,
and hosts of former colleagues and opponents
showed that there was unity of feeling in the
presence of coming death. To the family
assembled in the castle were added the grandchildren, and little Dorothy Drew was seen
reading with grave interest one of the bulletins
about her dying grandfather.

Thus went the bright though sad hours of
Wednesday. "Then came still evening on,"
and still the sufferer lingered. One of the
servants who had been absent when the others
paid a last farewell to the master of the house,
was accorded the privilege of entering the
sick-room early on Thursday morning, and
his visit almost synchronised with the departure of Mr. Gladstone. It was just five o'clock
on Ascension morning that "the weary wheels
of life stood still." William Ewart Gladstone
was "out of the body with God," after eighty-
eight years of strenuous life.

For some minutes there was silence in the
death chamber, save for the sobs which came

unbidden. Then some brief prayers brought solace to the bereaved family as they gazed at him who had been their most precious possession, *their* hero as well as the world's, their leader and teacher and loved one. In the porch, full of happy memories of the Gladstone Golden Wedding, was posted at last the news for which the world waited. The bulletin, signed by Dr. Habershon, Dr. Dobie, and Dr. Biss, stated : " Mr. Gladstone passed peacefully away at five o'clock this morning."

Instantly there was a rush to the post-office, which had a special staff of telegraphists to meet the emergency of the case. Within a few minutes all parts of the world knew that William Ewart Gladstone had passed from life, amid the love, veneration, and respect of countless millions. Most of the daily newspapers came out promptly with special editions, and portraits and biographies of the deceased statesman commanded a ready sale. In the House of Commons Mr. Balfour moved briefly that the House should adjourn for the day, and that it should consider on the following day the question of a public funeral and the erection of a monument to him who had been the chief ornament of Parliament for more than half a century. Sir William Harcourt seconded the formal motion, and the House dispersed. Next afternoon there were fine tributes paid to Mr. Gladstone's memory by representatives of different sections of each House.

UNWIN BROTHERS,
PRINTERS.
LONDON AND WOKING.

01/P